MW01502553

# Buffalo Confessions

# Sins, Secrets, and Atonement

*Patricia Ann Butler*

This is the last in a Series of contemporary novels written about the renaissance occurring in Buffalo, New York. and the people responsible for some of this renewal.

Buffalo has a unique history as a major city on Lake Erie, one of the Great Lakes. It borders Canada, and is the starting point for the Erie Canal.

The four previous novels by the author, dealt with the actions and reactions of people who worked, thrived, and helped others achieve their dreams in Western New York.

This novel is more concerned with the lives of some of the characters revealed to the reader through the musings of Father Rob Sullivan, the main persona who connects most of the characters in these works. His friendship, help, caring, and faith unites the characters in these five novels together, forever.

The four previous novels, in order, can be found at Amazon.com, by searching for the author, Patricia Ann Butler:
*The Lions of Buffalo*
*Wintering in Buffalo*
*Worth in Buffalo*
*The Unseen World of Buffalo*

This is a work of contemporary fiction. Apart from well-known people, events, and locales that figure in the narrative, all names, places, characters and incidents are products of the writer's imagination or used fictitiously. Any resemblance to current events or locales, or living persons, is entirely coincidental.

This final novel, set in Buffalo, NY, is dedicated to all who have flourished in this City of Good Neighbors. Thank you, all, for enjoying reading about places you know and love.

# Chapter 1

Next week, this congregation will be celebrating my 50th year of being a priest. Looking around, the people in the pews are all smiling, awaiting my homily. They weren't always smiling when I heard their failings in the dark wooden confessionals whenever their souls needed cleansing and absolution. Some were in agony. Some were miserable, and some were just plain embarrassed or ashamed. I hope to have brought some spiritual comfort and relief to all who entered my confessional, with the name plaque above it: *Reverend R. Sullivan.*

"Who am I to judge?" My papal boss, Francis I, has admonished this from the Vatican. Who am I to judge, indeed? My life hasn't exactly been all virtue. I have fallen off the morality wagon many times during my 75 years on this earth. I will reflect upon this fact in the week before the Golden Anniversary of my Ordination. Right now, I have to preach to my congregation:

*My Dear Brothers and Sisters in Christ,*
*Today I stand before you in this pulpit, full of humility. I am filled with joy that I was born to a sonofabitch of a father and a wimp of a mother who made it possible for me to live a life full of material riches. My poor sister died before she was mature enough to leave our family's den of thieves, and I still miss her, terribly. Who knows what I might have become if the judge presiding over my delinquency case hadn't decided I needed discipline instead of jail.*

*I never really thought about this before. Guess it's because I love being a priest. And...I love sinners. Mostly, I love being God's Pardoner. Through me, God's mercy on earth is brought forth to all of you, before death. No mortal sin will condemn someone to hell if I am reached out to first, for penance and absolution.*

Of course, this is **not** the sermon I delivered. I didn't want or need to confess my own sins and guilt to my parishioners and friends. They did not possess the power of sacramental forgiveness. I would reflect on my personal short-comings before next week's *Golden Gala*. I will go into retreat to confront my private demons. I wanted to be purified before accepting any congratulations on a life well-lived. I need to find repentance for my sins, first.

Looking around at my fellow-sinners, I began my actual sermon:

"My Dear Friends in Christ,

Next week you have decided to honor me for the privilege of ministering to your souls. You know my objections. However, I was unfairly induced to accept this honor by the promise of a great banquet, replete with all my favorite foods. Honestly, there isn't one food I cannot be tempted with, except, perhaps, pickled beets. Please, do not laugh. You know me well."

It was one of my strengths as a parish priest, that I did come to know many of my flock on a personal level. Other Christian sects and Jewish religions had this attribute as well. They knew who they were ministering to. I wanted that same kind of relationship, especially since we are not allowed spouses as priests in the Roman Catholic Church.

"I also know you well," I continued. "For fifty years, we have gone through the entire Ten Commandments, the Seven Deadly Sins, and, if I am counting correctly, ten United States presidents. We are on our eleventh, the 45th, and find ourselves fighting with each other over moral issues, as well as economic, military, environmental, educational, and security ones.

How did we come so far to become so far apart? I don't have the answer. I can only pray for peace. But, I also pray that next week, at the Golden Anniversary of our union, we can put our differences aside and celebrate how successful we have become in making our city great again. Looking around, I see men and women who have worked hard, together, to welcome refugees, to raise money for keeping our landmarks safe, and who have brought neighborhoods back into solvency, enabling Buffalo's true re-birth as a great city. We have sinned, but we have also practiced the Golden Rule of loving our neighbors as ourselves. I have also personally witnessed many of you practice the Eight Beatitudes and Corporal Works of Mercy. In my eyes, it all evens out.

I am proud to be a citizen here, as well as a spiritual guide.

Thank you, for all you have done, and all you continue doing. Let us celebrate during this Mass; God's purpose in bringing us together at this point of time and in this specific place on the Great Lakes. Let us offer each other a true sign of peace even before the *Lord's Prayer* today."

There was loud murmuring as each of my friends in Christ offered each other the sign of peace. Would that the sign could always be put into practice, but...I acknowledge our human frailty. We are neither angels nor demons.

Regarding my flock, I was grateful that they were and are under my care. I love them all, dearly...warts and all

I dismissed my congregation and bid them farewell after Mass.

Before entering the rectory, a stranger tapped my shoulder and asked if I had a minute. He looked about my age, perhaps at the beginning of his 70's. He also looked familiar. Of course, I couldn't place him right away, as I have met hundreds of people. Many people are easy to forget, but some are not. It's strange that my sense of smell conjures up more memories than my eyes, which can be deceived by the passage of time.

I asked the stranger to follow me into the office rectory. The minute of my time he had asked for was to take up more than that. It brought up years of my life, especially from my youthful past.

## Chapter 2

We settled in the rectory office. I assumed this was a new parishioner, preparing to register at St, Luke's, or perhaps a donor, wishing to contribute to the attached mission.

"Sorry for the unscheduled intrusion, Father. I would have called for an appointment, but my case is finally cracking open."

He handed me his card. It read:
*Detective Martin Foster; Niagara Falls, New York; 716-824-9790.*

"Are you here on official or spiritual business, Detective Foster?"

There were times the police sought my help in providing insight into some neighborhood crime. I could rarely be of assistance.

"A little of both," he smiled. He was in his early 70's's, I assumed, from his gray hair and weathered face. I noticed he had a facial structure indicating Native American ancestors. He was tall and in good shape, indicating frequent work-outs. I might have enjoyed being a detective, myself. if it wasn't for my eventual priestly vocation. I enjoyed solving puzzles, figuring out conundrums, and predicting how people would act and react in mystery novels. I was keenly interested in what this detective was looking for in this boring little corner of the world.

"Would you mind answering a few questions, Father Sullivan?" he asked, setting his cell phone on my desk, ready to record.

I cleared my throat. "I would be happy to, as long as the rule of confession isn't violated."

"I understand. I just need some background to fill in some of the missing blanks in my investigation."

"May I ask the nature of this investigation, Detective?"

"Of course. It's complicated, but thirty years ago, when I first became a detective, I was assigned a unique murder case. It involved a victim who was murdered but her body was moved to the Indian Reservation up in Lewiston. Since my mother was Indian, my superiors assumed I could more easily access information from the Indian sovereign nation."

I felt smug that my assumption as to this man's age and heritage was correct.

"Please continue, Detective. I don't recall reading anything about this. It was so long ago. Time flies, but a murder, and I believe you're going to inform me it's still unsolved, would have been safely stored in my memory vault."

"It was solved, actually. But, the evidence was lacking to convince a jury that the person, I believe committed it, could be charged."

"You're still looking for evidence?"

"I think I have enough of it now, but I need to connect some more dots."

"How can I possibly help?"

"You may have the clue as to why this poor young woman was murdered. Or, as I believe, was accidentally killed, and taken to the Reservation to cover up the accident and make it look like a murder."

"Why in the world would someone want an accident to appear to be murder?'

"Ah…that's where you come in, Father. Someone had to have a motive for covering up the accidental death. Someone had to have a reason to make sure no one knew about this young woman's connection to himself or herself."

"You're asserting that this connection is with someone who had something to lose if it was public knowledge."

"Exactly. I know you cannot name names. But, I think if we put our heads together, with your insight into human nature, and my experience with desperate acts people perform, we can come up with a plausible motive, and I can finally solve this murder that's been haunting me all these years."

"It sounds intriguing, I admit. But why did you choose me? I'm sure you could have asked a criminal psychologist to assist you."

He hesitated, but decided against bluffing. "I'm fairly certain that someone you know is involved, Father. He or she may not be the person responsible for the actual death of this woman, but I'm betting there is direct link between this person and the actual event when the death occurred."

"And you are so obsessed with this case because it's the only one you've left unsolved?"

"That's a part of it," he admitted. He took a deep breath, leaned forward and stated, "That young woman was my step-sister. So, I have more than a professional obligation to solve it. No one in the Department knew that, or I never would have been assigned the case. I didn't even know it, till I started the investigation."

"I don't understand."

"I think you know how people can hide their secret lives from the public and even from their own families and friends. There's always a way to lead more than one life."

He was correct. I have heard people confess this very fact, more than a few times. I even knew that my own father had quite a few secret lives.

"My father," Detective Foster continued, "was legal counsel to the Tuscarora Tribe. My mother was a member of the tribe, very beautiful, and when she married my white-Anglo father, they moved into a beautiful home in Lewiston, over-looking the Niagara Escarpment. Apparently, this wasn't enough for him. He cheated on my mother, as I learned from letters I found after her passing. My mother's sister, my Aunt Lucille, was a cocktail waitress at the Towne Casino in Buffalo. She frequently saw my father being overly-affectionate with a number of women. My aunt warned my mother that my father was being unfaithful. Her letters encouraged my mother to leave him. She said there was a home waiting for her and us kids at her home in Fort Erie, Ontario."

"Obviously, your mother wasn't persuaded to leave your father."

"Yes, and we kids had no idea what was going on. We had a stable childhood, even though we didn't see our father at the dinner table every night."

"Isn't that Club part of the mob history in Buffalo?"

"Yes. My father had a thing for women he wasn't married to. He usually baited his trap with promises of legal favors. He wined, dined, and made them feel important. He set them up with great jobs and took them on extravagant trips. Then he dumped them. That's why my mother never left him. She told my aunt that these girls were mere toys to him. Diversions. He always came back home and took care of us. She even told my aunt that it was acceptable for men to have women on the side, while their wives were pregnant, as having intercourse then could harm the child. My mother had four children. My father had more mistresses than four for sure. But why am I going off topic like this. Seems like you're too good a listener, Father Sullivan."

I laughed to ward off his embarrassment of getting so personal. "Hey, if you can't open up to a priest, who else can you rely on to get such cheap therapy from?"

He visibly relaxed.

"To lend credence to your mother's logic, many men, even men in the Bible were able to lay with women other than their wives because of Old and New Testament rules regarding sex, especially during menstruation and pregnancy. Read *The Red Tent* to understand a woman's perspective on this double standard."

"I'm not one for reading much, but my mother said *Men and women are different animals. It's a miracle when the two can lie down together.*"

"I like to think of it as a great blessing," I smiled., encouraging him to continue his personal story. "Your mother must have talked to you about your father's dalliances before she passed."

"Yes. My father was already dead. My mother told me where to find her letters and told me why she never accepted my Aunt Lucille's invitation to come live with her. She also told me other things which helped me discover my step-sister."

"Then, you had never met her when she was alive?"

"I did, but never knew we were related. She even went to the same high school I did."

"Did you go to La Salle?"

"I did. And the girl had her mother's last name. Apparently, my father had an affair with her mother after her father died. The girl used her mother's maiden name, so it took a while before I could connect all the family trees."

"Did you even find out the girl's father's name?"

"I did. But before I tell you, I think you should hear my father's name."

"Do I know him? Doesn't he have your last name?"

"Do you know Jason Lloyd Daniels?"

I swallowed hard. This was getting complicated. "I do. He was a business associate of my father. He was his legal advisor."

"*Jason Lloyd Daniels* is my father's name. My mother gave us her maiden name, *Foster* to protect us from the Press and from my father's business associates."

"My father assured us that Mr. Daniels was strictly a business acquaintance, and his ties to the Magaddino family didn't involve him."

"That's why I'm here, Father Sullivan. Judith Lee Silvers-Daniels was my half-sister."

I could feel the blood draining from my head. It felt like I was being dragged backwards through a violent time tunnel.

"Judith Lee? I muttered. "I knew her in high school. We dated in our Junior Year."

"Yes, I found that out, recently, going back through Yearbooks and interviewing her old friends that are still alive and in the area. You went to Canisius, but you and she went to the Roswell Benefit Ball together and were even crowned its King and Queen."

"When did you find out you were related to her?"

"DNA during the autopsy matched my father's. He was murdered, Father Sullivan, and the woman's body was unclaimed so we did a run-down on DNA data."

"This is getting very intense, Detective Foster. Your father was murdered?"

"One of the results of displeasing the head mob honcho as a *made man.* In 1957, you may recall a big Mob gathering was to take place just outside Binghamton in Apalachin. They were planning on taking over the entire USA economy. Construction, Labor Unions, trucking, clothing, food…the whole works. The Feds got there just in time to arrest 58 mobsters. My father was thought to be one of the tipsters. He was gunned down, with no indictments, and no leads as to who killed him. By 1989 there were 45 *m*ade men in Western New York. That's where I found the connection. In 1980, Judith was 37 years old. That's when Union members started giving info to the FBI."

"You don't think Judith was involved with the mob?"

"No. Her parents were dead. My mother was dead. And no one was even around to claim her body."

"So, what does the mob even have to do with all of this?"

"All boils down to greed. The Indians were talking about building a gambling casino in Niagara Falls after the Indian Gaming Regulatory Act of 1988. As of 2011., there were 460 gambling operations run by 240 tribes with an annual revenue of $27 billion."

I was shocked. "That's annual revenue?"

"Correct. You can imagine how many others wanted in on this cash bonanza."

"I can see the mob salivating. They obviously wanted to influence politicians to legalize gaming."

"For sure. People have always gambled. Games of chance are as old as mankind. The Lottery opened the door to legalized gambling in New York State. And when the chance came for them to make billions from casino gaming…well you know that there are more than ten non-Indian places to gamble just in our State. The newest one is in Schenectady and took just over a year to build."

"This is interesting, Detective. But where does poor Judith come in…or rather go out?"

"I have to believe that Judith was engaged to a persuasive politician who was against legalizing the casino industry in Niagara Falls. I believe Judith was in the cross-fires of a hit where the politician was killed, and Judith was an innocent victim of the gun-fire,"

"But why was her body taken to the Res?"

"To make it look like the Indians had murdered her and make it look like the tribe was violent and shouldn't be 'allowed to run a casino."

"And…?" I was confused.

"Someone had to think up the plan to defame the Indians and make it look like the only ones trustworthy enough to run the casino business was the government. I really mean corrupt politicians owned by the Mob."

"And…?"

"I believe you know the person who thought this plan up, and is partly responsible for Judith's death."

"I cannot divulge any information, Detective, as I told you before. I may have been privy to someone's confession."

"All I need from you, Father, is confirmation concerning my theory. Could the motive for Judith's death be a convenient way to disparage the Indians in order to get legalized gambling in Niagara Falls as the personal piggy bank for corrupt politicians and mobsters?"

I thought for a second, before plainly stating, "Yes."

I had a feeling this was going to get me involved with things I knew nothing about.


# Chapter 3


How could I possibly think of anything else, after Detective Foster had left? Everyone connected with Judith's death is dead themselves. I hope he found closure in my agreement of the possible motive for his half-sister's body being moved to the Reservation from where she and her fiancé were gunned down in Buffalo. He didn't know that Judith had come to confession, apparently a few months before her death.

When she entered the confessional box, I immediately recognized her unique scent: Ivory soap laced with bubble gum. It had been over 50 years since we had dated, when I had breathed in her freshness, but I have a strong scent memory. Many of my old sweaters still emanated the scent of *Beechnut* gum I had chewed incessantly when I was going through cigarette withdrawal 25 years ago. The sweaters were saturated with essence of peppermint.

I could go on about how I associate persons I know whose unique scents have been imprinted on my olfactory neurons, but at this moment, I will try to recall Judith's confession.

*Bless me, Father, for I have sinned.*

But instead of listing her sins and the number of times she committed them since her last confession, she immediately sought my counsel. I often heard moral problems and tried to help the poor souls work out their dilemmas by letting them talk, anonymously. Many times, they found their own answers this way. Judith did have a serious moral dilemma.

*I haven't any new sins, Father, but I need advice. When I was in my 20's, I hung with a wild crowd. One of the guys got me pregnant...not once...but twice. I miscarried the first time, but had an abortion the second time. I felt so awful about this that I finally broke up with the jerk and broke away from the group. I got my act together and went back to school for court stenography. I met my current fiancé then. He's wonderful, but he's also in politics. He's a lawyer who wants to run for City Council. The problem is...if the newspapers get ahold of my personal life, it could be a bad influence on his campaign. He doesn't know about my past. He thinks I'm a sweet innocent young woman who never found the right guy and that's why I wasn't married yet. He wasn't wrong about not finding the right guy. No offense, Father, but most guys I've known are self-absorbed douche bags. They may look good, but they treat women like stuff they can step all over. They must have missed the class on how to be gentlemen, so they have no class. I don't buy the excuse that it's all because of women's lib. They don't have common courtesy and that's not because of women's lib.*

She didn't know I was aware of who she was, I think. But, she must have known my reputation as a fairly liberal cleric. The lines at my confessional were longer than the more conservative priests.

I listened to her patiently, but had to get to the crux of her problem, which she was obviously avoiding.

*So the problem you're facing is you're afraid your past might negate your present and future with this man?*

*Exactly, Father. I don't know if I should tell him about my past, or pray he never finds out and just shut my mouth.*

*What's your gut feeling?*

*I want to have an honest relationship with him, but I'm so afraid that my long ago past will catch up and kill his love for me, not even mentioning his respect.*

*Do you trust this man?*

*Yes, he's the most honest person I've ever met. He wants to get into politics to clean up all the corruption he sees every day in Court.*

*Do you think he would understand that all your past mistakes happened many years ago, and that you've changed?*

*I would hope so. He's very compassionate and has never had a serious relationship before, either.*

*Are you willing to take the chance that he will still love you for who you are now, in spite of your past?*

There was silence for a minute. I knew she was wrestling mightily with her conscience for an answer she could live with.

Finally, I heard take a deep breath, and knew she had come to an acceptable conclusion.

*I guess if he really loves me as much as he says he does, and he's the great kind of guy I think he is, I'll have to find a way to at least give him a chance to hear what I need to tell him about my past mistakes.*

*That's a logical decision. But, is your heart ready to accept that he may decide you're not the person for him?*

*I'll work on that. But for now, living in fear that he'll find out about everything from the newspapers, or a political enemy would be worse. What's my penance, Father?*

*I think deciding on what the right thing to do will be penance enough. Good luck and God Bless. May the Lord be with you to give you strength and bring you peace.*

Of course, back then there was no Internet to probe into every nook and cranny of a person's past. She could easily have taken her chances that her past would never be revealed. I had a feeling that she would come clean to the man she loved, and trust that they would work out the possible political fall-out together.

Two weeks later, I read about the young politician who was gunned down after having dinner at Roseland Restaurant on Rhode Island. The young woman he was with had disappeared.

I read a few weeks later that the unidentified body of a young woman was found on the Tuscarora Indian Reservation. The news article quoted a prominent politician who emphatically stated that this was proof that the Indians should not be allowed to open up and run a gambling casino which might promote more murders and crime. Certain police must have been paid off to close the investigation. The mob was able to reach into legal agencies in order to extend their illegal activities. They were able to fly under the radar for quite a while. This all would have been pushed under the rug and would have disappeared. But, I too, had some connections.

A friend of mine in the Police Department confirmed to me that that the young woman was identified as Judith Lee Silvers. There was no mention of who her birth father was."

Of course, Detective Foster had told me. It was my father's legal counsel, Jason Lloyd Daniels, who was still a prominent attorney in Niagara County at the time of the murders.

My thoughts were interrupted by the land line's harsh ring. The rectory office still had a black rotary desk phone. I used it during office hours, but relied on my cell for caller ID.

"St. Luke's," I answered. "Father Robert Sullivan."

"You must have your cell off, Rob. I tried calling you for an hour."

It was Lenore. "You could have just walked over, you know. Your office is a few yards away." She ran the Mission attached to the rectory.

"I'm too busy planning your big party," she laughed. Lenore was an amazing woman who was not only a wonderful interior designer, but she and her husband, organized and ran the Mission which housed and trained refugees. She was also one of my best friends.

"I don't really care, Lenore. Do what you want. I didn't even want this bash in the first place."

"Just shut your mouth...*please*. You're going to have a party and that's that." Lenore was used to giving orders. Now that I think about it, she and her other women friends are also bossy. They tell me what I have to do all the time. It's like having a harem of wives. I chuckled to myself at this revelation.

"Don't laugh, Rob. I'm on deadline and have to call the caterer to finalize the menu."

"I'm confident that the food choices will be fine. Just not too fancy."

"You're the one who said you wanted roast beef, chicken wings, hot dogs, pizza and apple pie. Is that plebian enough for you?"

"Glad you took my requests seriously."

"You might not have shown up if I hadn't."

"I'm a true Buffalonian, Lenore. I've ministered to Buffalonians. We should eat fine Buffalo cuisine."

"Fine. But there may be many grouchy hungry people there."

"If the dieting ladies don't want to eat, there'll just be more for the true gourmands."

"Lots of men are watching their cholesterol too, nowadays, you know."

"I'll grant dispensation for one afternoon. So finalize the delicacies already."

"Are you sure you want the polka band, too?"

"Absolutely. That should cure the grouchiness. No one can sit still and not smile during a rousing polka. Make sure there's plenty of beer, wine, and krupnik."

"You're from Irish parents, right?"

"Yep. But, my heart is Italian, my love of nature is German, and my joy is Polish."

"What part of you is Irish?"

"My sadness for the human race."

"I have to laugh." I could hear good nature in her voice. Lenore could be intense at times, but her sense of humor was flawless.

"There. Now you know how I roll. I'm a well-seasoned Pastor with all of Buffalo's ethnic groups, I wouldn't be a true Buffalonian if I wasn't."

"Preaching to the choir, Rob. I run the Mission, remember?"

Indeed, I did. Lenore and her husband have worked miracles on the East Side.

"Do you think the Central Terminal will be large enough for this bash?"

"Sarcasm. Now I know you're into this. The Terminal will be decorated with gold, Rob."

"Good. I'm satisfied you decided to include a fund-raiser to save the grand old place from the wrecking ball of supposed progress."

"Again…if we didn't, you wouldn't have shown up."

"Glad we're on the same page."

"Always."

"So, I'll see you at the Bach Birthday Bash tomorrow at Kleinhans?"

"Looking forward to it. I bet you're looking forward to the pre-concert dinner Tina's planned for us."

"Really? You have to ask? The only problem is I'll have to take home a doggie bag. If I eat too much before the concert, I may very likely fall asleep in the middle of it."

"Good point. I won't tell you what the menu is, but warn you to eat lightly during the day."

"Thanks for the warning…but how about a hint?"

"One of your favorites."

"That isn't helpful. I love everything Tina cooks up."

"Okay…it's one of your favorite Polish treats."

"I'm already licking my chops."

"Ha-ha. Nice try. No more hints."

"You're too quick for me, Lenore. See you tomorrow at 5 o'clock."

"One more thing, Rob."

"Hurry up. It's time for my nap."

"Who was that man you were walking with to the rectory after Mass today?"

My guard was up. "Why? Do you know him?"

"No reason. I think I've seen him at the Mission before, but never had a chance to speak with him."

"It's a long story. I'll explain at dinner tomorrow."

"No hints?"

"Now you know how it feels, my dear."

I kept it light with Lenore, but my mind was still reeling from my conversation with Detective Foster about Judith's death. After my nap, I'd have to think about how much I would divulge to Lenore and Tina. Or rather…how much I could keep from them.

## Chapter 4

It's annoying when I can't turn off my brain for a well-deserved rest. I couldn't nap because I kept returning to the past. Thanks a lot Detective Foster and Lenore. I remember, vividly, Lenore's confession to me when she was 12 years old:

*I know it's wrong to hate, Father, but I hate two people very much. What makes it worse is they're my parents.*

*But aren't your parents in heaven, my child?*

*Probably, more like hell. They were two drunks, Father. They made my brother, my grandmother, and my life hell when they were alive. Now that they're dead, I still hate them.*

*How does this hate make you feel?*

*That's why I'm here. It makes me feel terrible.*

*Do you think your hate hurts or punishes your parents?*

*No. They're wherever they are. Gram said they must be in Purgatory having their sins burned off. She doesn't think they're in hell.*

*Your grandmother was very wise. She made sure you and your brother were safe and well-cared for when she was alive. She even made sure you would be taken care of after she died.*

*I know. I love her with all my heart, even though she's in heaven.*

*How does this feeling of love make you feel?*

*It feels good, I feel warm and peaceful when I think of Gram.*

*What do you think would happen to you if you let the hate you have for your parents go away?*

There was silence in the confessional. I knew young Lenore would begin to think more with her mind, and less with her anger.

*I think not hating would make me feel better...almost kinda free.*

*So, does this hate hurt you more... or your parents?*

*It hurts me more.*

*So, what do you have to try and do every day?*

*Try to hate less and less instead of more and more.*

*It wouldn't hurt to try, would it?*

*I guess not. Then, I guess my penance is trying to throw away my hate.*

*I think that might make you feel better and more at peace. You don't have to feel the same way you do about your grandmother, but then you don't have to be all tangled up by the feelings you have for your parents either.*

I had the great privilege of watching Lenore grow up into a loving compassionate woman, free of hatred for her parents. She was free to love everyone, including herself, as she was not using her energy to hate.

I still couldn't nap after this memory faded, because another one from the past stepped up into its place. This one involved Tina and her confession of hate. Tina was coping with a grown woman's hatred when she entered my confessional:

*You know how my story goes, Father. I had a child out of wedlock, had an unfaithful husband, and hid my intense hatred for his emotional abuse even after he died. I can't help feeling that God punished me for this hatred when I had to live through the tragedy of another death situation last year. This was so painful, that I even admitted to you that I hated God for allowing this tragedy to happen. Do you think I am being punished for my hatred?*

*I do not believe God works that way, my dear. I truly believe God is large enough to let our puny feelings dissolve before they even reach Him, even if they are as strong as hate.*

*Then what about love? Does God consider human love to be so inconsequential as well?*

*Really? I believe whether we love or hate Him is of no consequence. He is more concerned with how much we love or hate each other.*

*Then how about the Commandment to love the Lord thy God above all else?*

*It may be that this love is more faith and trust than love. We prove our love to God and to each other by actions, not words, not even prayers. The best way to show true love is to act lovingly.*

*I think you're telling me that all the sadness I've been through is not God punishing me, but more testing me?*

It was rewarding when someone got the abstractions I was always doling out.

*If you trust and have faith that these things happened for a reason, even one we can't comprehend, then this must show God more love than just saying it. Your acceptance shows him you trust that He loves you.*

*Strangely, this kind of makes sense. My husband always told me he loved me, while acting out a lecherous life till the day he died. And when horrible tragedy hit me without warning, I was in an emotional tailspin and thought I'd never get right side up again.*

*What helped you find your bearings?*

*My dear friends, their loving actions, and their faith that I would be okay, even if scarred deeply.*

*You trusted your friends?*

*I did.*

*Then trust that God can't dissolve your pain, but that He has faith that you will survive.*

*I think you're right, Father. I just needed to hear it out loud. I feel lighter…not so much weighed down with sadness. I guess I really just needed to hear it was alright to start being happy again.*

Tina is happy, now. She makes me happy, being her friend. Having a great cook as a friend doesn't hurt, but she has a very rewarding calling helping others. And tomorrow, she will help me make a pig of myself. I do hope there is pork on the menu. Lenore was cruel in not giving me a hint.

I don't care if people think my love of food is excessive. It's not the amount I eat; it's that the sense of taste is one of the pleasures priests are allowed to enjoy. Food can be, and is for me, very sensual: Tasting, smelling, seeing, savoring. A home-cooked meal is my loving mistress.

Tonight, I would have to fend for myself in the food department. Saturday was date night in the world. I usually took an evening stroll, by myself, along Miller Street to Broadway. Norm's still was a pizzeria where I'd get two slices, hear news of the neighborhood, then get a ride back to the rectory with a delivery boy or walk back myself, if the weather was okay. At home, I'd settle in to watch re-runs of my favorite Westerns: *The Rifleman, Gunsmoke, and Maverick.* These gems were like morality plays. Many themes of my sermons were mined from these great stories of the battle between goodness and evil.

I could smell the cheese, sauce, and pepperoni baking into a perfect pie of perfection a few houses away. My delight was abruptly interrupted by the crack of gunfire and the sight of two boys running out the door of the pizzeria.

Thankfully, I saw Norm run out soon enough, shouting. "Don't let me ever catch you lazy bastards near my place again. This isn't a toy gun, and next time it won't be used to just scare you, you scum of the earth. Oh Hi, Father Rob. I was just pulling your pizza out of the oven. Come on in."

"Trouble in Paradise?" I asked, stepping into the mouth-watering plain pizza pick-up place, where sit-down wasn't encouraged.

"Not really. Rose, here, was waiting on those two bums, when she gave me the *look.* She meant to warn me they were up to no good. I took out my little air pistol and shot in the air. The two got the message and ran off. How's the pizza?"

"Great, as usual," I muttered, my mouth still stuffed with the goodness of this Polish-Italian pizza man. "So, what's the news?"

"Not too much. I'm going to go to your Golden Anniversary, as a guest, this time, not as your pizza man. Lenore told me she ordered pizzas and wings from La Nova and not to be offended. Of course, I told her I wasn't. Too big an order for my little place. Besides, my cousins own the place."

"Nice to know there's no pizza rivalry."

"Hey, Father, you know me. I work hard, put out a great product, and make enough honest money to keep a roof over my head."

"And the side jobs? They probably pay for your winter get-a-ways?"

"Yeah. A little gambling business on the side hurts no one. If it wasn't for me, and the daily numbers, lots of my neighbors would be lost. I'm, right here and honest with their wagers."

"Did you know those boys, Rose?" I asked the lovely young woman taking the phone orders.

"Yeah. They're local losers. Can't even join a gang, 'cause they have too much sense."

"That makes them losers?"

"To the gangs. I think they're losers 'cause they have smarts but they won't use them to get out of this dead-end neighborhood. I graduated from high school with them. We started at Buff State together, but they dropped out after the first semester. Told me it was stupid stuff they were learnin' that couldn't be used in the real world. I know it was too hard for 'em. They were too proud to admit they needed tutorin'."

"What do they do now?"

I suspected they would not even be able to join a gang. The gangs wanted dumb followers, with a lot of greed for easy money and a longing to belong.

"I'm pretty sure the gang told them if they held up this place, they might be worthy to become members. So when they walked in, then put their hands in their jacket pockets, I gave Norm the eye. I don't think they had real guns, but better safe than sorry."

"I even offered one of 'em a job, delivering" Norm was disgusted. "The jerk said *No* because he knew he'd be held up by those gangster punks every time he went out to deliver."

"So, they make money, how?"

"They do odd jobs and work on cars," Rose sighed. "It's a shame, 'cause they're both church boys and go with their mothers every week."

"Hope you'll be at my anniversary bash, Rose."

"Already have a snatched outfit, Father. Everyone is excited about something this nice happening in the hood, and for free."

"Snatched?"

Rose laughed. "Gotta keep current, father. The new *cool.*"

"Thank the Lord I at least know what *cool* means."

"Have a great evening, Father," Norm waved. "The usual cowboy flicks?"

"That's correct, pardner. Headin' back to the ranch."

I walked out using my best John Wayne swagger. They were laughing at my poor attempt.

# Chapter 5

Half-way down the block, Antoine jumped in front of me. He was one of the would-be robbers, who had tried to perform a mock heist. I didn't tell Norm or Rose I had recognized him.

"I'll walk you home, Father. This ain't the greatest neighborhood."

"So why are you still in it, Antoine? And why were you going to try and rob Norm?"

"I knew you saw me. Sorry. My cousin, Marcus, convinced me to help him with it so he could become initiated as a gang banger."

"You have an awful lot of cousins, Antoine."

"Part of the African-American culture," he smiled. "We don't believe too much in birth control or abortion."

I realized that there was a popular conspiracy theory that the government was trying to sterilize the black race, in order to eliminate them from *the white race only USA*. There were many taboos associated with birth control and abortion dating back to slavery issues.

"When are you going back to school, Antoine?"

"C'aint. My Mom needs me here to help her support the twins and Jamal.

"Dad's not in the picture?"

"Unless jail is the family album you're referring to."

"Sorry." I didn't want to ask what his father was in jail for. Most of the men in this neighborhood had children they couldn't support because of criminal records, or wouldn't because they had children from more than one mother and left it up to Social Service to do their parenting.

"What if I make you a win-win proposition, Antoine?"

"I'm listenin'"

"What if I send your mother a weekly check to help with your siblings. Then give you a monthly allowance so you could pick up your scholarship and continue your education?"

"Why would you even think 'bout doin' this?"

"Don't look a gift horse in the mouth," I said, trying to make it look like he was helping me out instead of doling out charity to him. "I believe in chipping away at mountains, one piece at a time."

"I'm one of your pieces, then," Antoine smiled.

"Could be," I explained. "One person back in school and successful, shows others it's possible to get a fair shake in a rotten system."

"But, how are others goin' to afford their stake? They're all in the same situation as me."

"Great logic, Antoine. See? I knew you have smarts. Let me further entice you by bribery. If you stay in school with a 2.5 to 3.5 average, I'll sponsor another kid and his family, for every C or B you earn."

"What if I have a few A's?"

"Then I'll sponsor three for every A you earn."

"If you're serious…I'm in."

"Great. Thanks for walking me back to the rectory. Stop by tomorrow, and we'll work out the details." Hope I left Antoine with more hope than he had when he had the crazy idea to hold up Norm's. Money can be used for many things. I wondered what will happen when encrypted funds like *bit coin* become the norm. Will crime go away because there won't be any more currency exchanged in cash? I was feeling grateful that I may be gone before all these changes take place. Hopefully, someone smart enough to know how bit coin worked could transfer my inheritance into useful funds.

Many people think that with my connection to Lenore and the Mission, I have access to County and State funds. In truth, there is a pot of money allotted to the Mission from government sources. But, in my case, I have a trust fund. Quite a large one, left to me by my father. We didn't see eye to eye when I was young. We managed to reconcile while he was dying of cancer.

The big "C" is the variable in everyone's life. It's interesting that scientists now seem to believe that sheer luck, or rather bad luck, has more to do with getting it than genes, diet, or life-style. Cells mutate as randomly as a throw of dice. I use this theory many times now, when counseling someone stricken with this disease. It's easier to reconcile a turn of bad luck than trying to discourage someone from trying to figure out how the person may have prevented it from occurring. We humans have got to firmly understand that in life, everything is a gamble. And the only way to cope with a bad deal is to trust that God is on our side and trust His way is the best chance we have against eternal damnation. We control very little in life. We can only make decisions we think may be the right ones. My father never learned this. He tried to control everyone and everything, including my future. He didn't like my becoming a priest, one bit; until he was on his death bed, begging for forgiveness.

That's why, I needed to help Antoine and his ilk. The die is cast against them because of society's prejudices. He doesn't have a biological father in his life. Sometimes I have to be a surrogate dad. I love it. But, when my *children* don't listen to my advice, it bothers me. Guess there's more of my own father in me than I care to admit.

The TV escape route was the one I sought right now. I was bone tired. A re-run of one of the great *Rifleman* series was just what I needed. Chuck Connors played a great father to his son in the old Wild West. Of course, I fell asleep, in ten minutes.

At first, I thought the TV had awakened me, but it was the harsh ringing of my cell. I had forgotten to silence it. It was a police friend of mine, Sean Rogers.

"Father Rob, you better come down to the county hospital. A kid's been shot and is calling for you."

"Another one? I thought the violence had died down."

Not for this kid. Name's Antoine. Says he knows you."

## Chapter 6

"What the hell, Antoine. You just left me. Thank God it's your arm and not your head that's been hit. Sorry for the cuss."

"True, dat," he admitted, just as his mother came flying into the room.

"You better not be involved in that gang shit," she ran to his side, pushing me away with her hip, flinging herself at him.

"OW, MOM! Chill. I'm going to be fine. Get off me, and I was innocently walking home. Sorry 'bout this, Father Rob. My Mom's just showing her worry by acting all mad. Right here is Father Rob, the priest guy I told you 'bout, Mom. He's a minister."

"Sorry, Reverend. My apologies. This here almost grown man is going to be the death of me, yet."

"Maybe I can explain, Ma'am, how I hope to save his life and yours. Antoine, may I explain my proposition to you mother?"

"He nodded. "I was goin' to tell her tonight, anyway."

I explained my offer to Antoine's mother. She was thrilled.

"I knew the Lord wouldn't forget us," she proclaimed earnestly.

"He'll have a fighting chance away from this neighborhood. You better not mess this up, Twan, you hear?"

"Yes, Ma'am. Studying my brains out is better than having them blown out."

We planned that Antoine would be staying on campus, and his mother would be receiving a stipend from me, under the table, for two grand a month. Enough to cover her rent and some living expenses, and not too much to make her friends jealous and the government too nosy. We pledged to keep our mouths shut about this arrangement. They understood my trite comment, "Loose lips sink ships."

It was midnight before I was able to crawl back into dreamland. I had an early call, as confession would begin at 7:30 a.m., a short time before 8:00 a.m. Mass. I had a deep dreamless sleep, and was awake by 6:00 am, my usual.

I felt sleepy in the confessional box, but was sharply awakened by the person who entered almost immediately.

*"Bless me, Father. I'm the stupid fool who shot Antoine. I'm so sorry, but glad I aimed to hurt, not kill. That crazy-ass gang made me do it, because our plan to rob Norm's fell apart. Antoine knew it was me. He called me last night and told me he was going to disappear from this scene as soon as he was released. He said I should talk to you 'bout my situation. So here I am."*

*"Then you must be Marcus?"*

*"Yeah. And I am a sorry fool."*

*"How would you like me to help you?"*

*"Twan said you could help me disappear too."*

*"Did he say how?"*

*"Yeah...I mean Yes, Father. I'm ready to give it all another shot."*

*"Your best shot?"*

Silence...which was a good sign he was taking my offer seriously.

*"Yes, Father. I'd be grateful for your help."*

We made arrangements for him to meet me at the rectory later that afternoon to work out his details. My conscience was clear in donating my money to certain folks who wanted to better themselves without letting the government in on my arrangements. I'm not justifying my actions. But, if banks can be bailed out with no jail time imposed on the perpetrators of their crimes, then I can bail out poor people from poverty without fear of jail time as well.

I then celebrated Mass in a very humble, grateful mood. The Lord does work in mysterious ways. My ministry was greatly involved in helping my flock, if not understand this concept, at least accept it on faith, trust, and ho

# Chapter 7

Looking around at the daily Mass attendees, I saw the usual. There was one new person near the back. She was wearing a scarf; unusual since the weather was warm for late April, and women no longer needed a head covering in church. Maybe she was trying to protect her identity. This wasn't so unusual. I used to be pastor of a wealthy congregation on Delaware Ave. Lenore convinced me that I was more needed at the Mission church. She was right. But, many of my parishioners from the rich part of town came down to the East Side for confession. They craved forgiveness and atonement, but also needed anonymity. Many lawyers, judges, CEO's and bankers came here for confession. Usually, they donated heavily to the Mission as part of their self-imposed penance. It was a great way for them to ease their consciences and fill up the Mission treasury.

One comptroller had come confessing she was embezzling money from her employer to the tune of a few million dollars. Only recently had she begun to feel nervous. Her conscience wasn't affected, but her fear of being found out urged her to seek my advice. She knew I couldn't reveal her sin, and she didn't want to trust an outside therapist. I advised her to take a vacation to think about what she was doing. While she was away, the cooked books were reviewed by an outside source. She was indicted, found guilty, and now I visit her is prison. Ironically, she is relieved to have that monkey finally off her back. She advises her fellow inmates as to how to secure their financial futures. Of course, her advice is legal this time.

On my way back to the rectory, I could sense the woman with the scarf approaching me from behind. When I turned to acknowledge her, I almost fell to the ground. Detective Foster had whipped off the head scarf. He stood there grinning at my shock.

"What the...?"

"I know. It's not the most clever of disguises, but I wanted to see the people who go to you for confession. I see that one of kids who was in the car that shot at Antoine was there."

"So, you know Antoine?"

"I know everyone in this neighborhood, Father. I want to see who comes here from other neighborhoods."

"Aren't you retired."

"Aren't you?"

"Touche."

"Let's just say I want to tie up some loose ends. You know I can't arrest a dead person in connection to my step-sister, Judith's death. Whoever did it was politically joined with their black hearts to the Mob. I know you know that her father was a friend of your father. I also know you know your father had a lot of influence in the way things were done in Buffalo when we were both growing up, naively believing in peace and justice for all."

"Are you accusing my father, Detective, of having a hand in Judith's death?"

"No. I know that Jason Lloyd Daniels' grandson is running for political office next year. I want to make sure his election is not going to cause someone else's death."

"Why might that be?"

"I think the grandson, Jackson Daniels has some unsavory details in his past that might prevent him from taking office."

"It would be impossible for anyone to hide anything from the public nowadays." I countered.

"That's for sure. But, there might be someone still looking into his grandfather's past sins that might affect his grandchildren's futures"

"Are you frightened because of what you know?"

"Not exactly. I just have a hunch that something's wrong with the political scene as I see it. I want to find out what's going on."

"So, you came to church?" I laughed.

"It's the place where sinners come to find relief...and I assume, advice from their favorite confessor." Detective Foster was serious.

"I think you're giving too much credit to me for being the repository of all of the Buffalo community's wrong-doings. You have a dead-end here, Detective."

"Maybe. I only know that you know almost everyone in Buffalo who's been and still is rich and powerful. Unfortunately, the two types combined means someone is guilty of something."

"That's pretty cynical."

"Aren't you? Cynical...I mean, Father. You see human nature as much or more than I"

"To tell you the truth, I'm mostly tired. Right now, I need a nap. Maybe you could use one, too, Detective. You might wake up with a better perspective of the human race, if you weren't so tired."

# Chapter 8

Back at the rectory, after setting up Marcus's stipend to his family, I was able to finally take a well-deserved nap. There was no way I wanted to be grouchy and sleepy during the meal Tina was preparing for us before attending Bach's Bash at Kleinhans.

I played his *Brandenburg Concert #3*. There are a total of six movements which were never popular or even played during the composer's life in the 1700's. I loved them because they show how he integrated all the musical knowledge of the time and also glorified the divine harmony of the universe. There is always something new to be gleaned from his works, no matter how often they are heard. Bach's soul touches mine across the ages through my ears. His music soothes and inspires me. It's like God speaking to me. I was able to sleep soundly and wake up totally refreshed, looking forward to my evening meal with great friends

Lenore and I were riding together. I didn't own a car. No need. It freed me, actually. If I needed one for distant travel, I simply rented one.

"Tina's excited to see your reaction to the feast she's prepared for us," Lenore hinted.

"You are a great tease, my dear. I'm not going to beg for information. I'll know soon enough."

"Tina's son is back working for the government, you know?"

"Glad he found a someplace to use his talents. He's in Washington?"

"Yep. His Special Service experience is valuable for his State Department appointment. He wanted to be here for your Golden, but with the problems in the Capitol, he couldn't get away."

"Are you all set with the Trust Fund release of money for the two young men I told you about?"

"Ready, Sir Galahad. At least some problems are being solved in our corner of the world. Your list of young people making use of your money is admirably growing."

"That's what money is for. Can't leave it to the Church. I don't see much help it's offering to the people in the streets where gangs are recruiting every day."

"Aren't you afraid some gangster is going to get mad and target you for bagging their potential recruits?"

"Nah. They don't know it's this old guy who's causing them grief. They think it's some other drug pusher poaching them. They like to mug for their pictures on the Internet, looking like bad dudes. It would damage their creds, if they were pictured shooting a man like me instead of some bad competitor from their territory."

"Well, be careful, anyhow. You wouldn't be the first priest knocked off for lesser reasons."

"Ah, here we are at Tina's lovely loft, thanks to your decorating talent, Lenore."

"Why thank you. When are you going to let me into your den of iniquity? The rectory office is a hazard."

"Maybe next week, as a matter of fact. The dust is growing in layers, and the ceiling is way too high to clear the cobwebs."

"Really? This is great. I'll come by with some ideas."

"You don't waste time, do you?"

"You and I don't have that much more time to waste."

"Me, less than you."

"I was trying to be kind."

"Forget it. I know if the good Lord wants me sooner, rather than later, I'm ready."

"Well, we're not."

"It's not up to you, is it? *Miss Control the World.*"

"I know. I know. But the Mission is my world, and I do control it."

"And very well, I might add. I don't compliment you enough Lenore on how much your work has made a difference in so many lives that were once hopelessly helpless."

"I do have an issue I'd like to discuss after dinner."

"No problem, as long as it doesn't interrupt dessert."

"How do you know Tina's made dessert."

"Ha-Ha," I laughed, ringing the bell to Tina's loft, over-looking Lake Erie. The glorious aroma of pork wafted through the air, in greeting, as Tina opened the door with a flourish."

# Chapter 9

"Welcome to my humble abode."

Tina looked younger every time I saw her. Buffalo was doing her a world of good. I think her make-over that another friend had insisted on to rid her of her Southern matronly look, affected even her attitude. The fact that her young vibrant grand-daughter, Tia, lived near her didn't hurt either."

"You've read my mind, Tina. I was craving a pork dish."

"Then have a seat, and get ready for a treat of mock chicken."

"Huh? I un-mistakenly smell pork."

"I know. And it is. It's pork cubes on skewers that mimic chicken legs. Polish ingenuity when chickens were scarce and pork more accessible."

We sat down at her dining table, facing the lake. April is a changeable month, full of hope for a rebirth of green. The sun on the water sparkled with it. Too cool yet, for plein -air dining, a view of the water was very calming.

"Ready to eat, Rob?"

"You jest, indeed."

"I'm famished, too, Tina," Lenore added. "I haven't eaten anything yet, all day."

"Foolish child," I said, ogling the platter of mock chicken, swimming in gravy. There was also sweet and sour cabbage, garlic baby carrots, new spring baby potatoes, and home- made rye bread.

"Is this pleasing to your palate, your majesty," Tina smiled, knowing what my answer would be.

"What's for dessert?" I teased

"Apple pie, of course."

"Perfection," I muttered, stuffing my mouth with a cube of tender pork from a skewer, that melted in my mouth.

We enjoyed the wonderful feast, and I did not over-do, requesting a take-home plate to enjoy tomorrow. Tina had already prepared it, with enough for two more meals. My *girlfriends* always took good care of nourishing me. I usually had my meals in the Mission cafeteria, but home-made meals weren't in short supply, and were much appreciated. I have to admit, it gave my girls as much pleasure creating dishes for me to enjoy, as well.

We settled in Tina's lovely cozy living room around a gentle fire, enjoying our pie. Tina's pie crust was divinely flaky. After two satisfying bites, I asked Lenore to describe the issue with the Mission she had mentioned.

"Nothing too serious concerning the refugees we're serving now," she reported, "but I'm afraid the ban on new refugees is going to cause many families great concern. They're here waiting for new hope and also their family members and friends to join them in safety. Now, confusion and political intrusion is becoming an issue."

"How can we help?" Tina asked. She was and still is involved in helping new refugees find their way to the Mission.

"That Detective, Rob, who was in your rectory and at the Mission, seems to have been hired by some politician wanting ammunition to use in his bid for election to some kind of Buffalo office."

"Do you know the politician's name?"

"I believe he's the grandson of your father's old friend, Jason Lloyd Daniels."

I stopped my third pie bite in mid-air.

"What? Something the matter, Rob?" Tina asked, thinking I was offended by her scrumptious pie.

"Not with the pie, Tina. Jason Lloyd Daniels' grandson is running for public office?"

"Yes. Do you know him? His name is Jackson Daniels?" Lenore stated.

"I do," Tina answered. "Tia went on a few dates with him, when she was enrolled in Political Science at Canisius. She said he was fairly arrogant, though very good-looking."

"Did she change majors?" Lenore asked.

"Yes. She realized she could do more good in Biology. Her options in finding a worthwhile job improved when the Medical Corridor opened."

I listened to their banter about how so many new opportunities opened up with solar energy plants, medical research and such, that there should be no problem for young people finding jobs if they had the proper training in the right fields.

"Tina, thank you for the most delicious meal I've enjoyed in a while. You are a terrific chef. But, we should get going in order to make the Bach Bash on time."

"Car's already been called, Rob." Lenore was always on the ball.

"*The Brandenburg Concertos* are a perfect selection for Spring," Tina commented.

"They certainly are full of lively lilts," I agreed.

"We can only hope and pray that the cuts in culture are going to be vetoed. Buffalo's a sports town for sure. But, music, dance, poetry, drama, art, movies and so many lovely ways to express the human spirit are also well-attended and need public support as well as new stadiums and high-priced athletes." Lenore was agitated.

"More work for us to fund-raise for if these cuts are made," I advised. "We can do it. People in Buffalo are always generous with supporting the Arts."

# Chapter 10

The car dropped us off right in front of the entrance to Kleinhans Music Hall. Another plus of not having a car to park. I was in a great mood; well-fed in body, awaiting musical nourishment to my soul.

"Bet you didn't think I had an ounce of culture in my bones, Father Rob."

I turned to see Detective Foster smiling Cheshire-like in my face.

"I never pre-judge, Detective. Nice to see you again, so soon. Are you here by yourself?"

He laughed. "A priest wouldn't lie, would he?" He had noticed my sarcastic tone. "I'm afraid I've never married. Tied to my job. No space for family life. Like you, somewhat, Father."

I introduced him to Lenore and Tina. Lenore couldn't hide her amazement.

"Are you stalking us, Detective?" she demanded.

"I'm here to enjoy the intricacies of Bach's genius," he replied calmly. "I often play his music when trying to solve other intricate mysteries."

"Such as?" I asked.

"There are so many I've tried to solve in my career. Thank God, Bach was prolific. Sometimes I've been successful, and at times, not so much. There were too many loose ends."

"Are you still trying to tie up some loose ends, tonight?" I asked.

"No, Father. Tonight, I clear my mind. Tomorrow something unclear may surface bright and shiny, luring me to follow it."

"Is the Mission one of your fishing spots, Detective?" Lenore was being sarcastic, now.

"I think I've been able to fish out some information on my last visit, Lenore. You run a wonderful needed shelter. There is nothing I would do to harm your endeavors."

This placated her considerably. "Well...the next time you visit, you're welcome as a guest to tour the entire facility."

"Thank you. I'll be sure to take you up on that invite."

"The warning bell was ringing. It was time to forget the world, and let our spirits be lifted to the heavens with divine music.

# Chapter 11

The concert was superb. We have so many venues today for spiritual nourishment. The Arts can't be ignored as a frivolous past-time. All civilizations flourish that recognize this truth. Take this glorious music hall. It used to be the site of a huge mansion, owned by a very wealthy Buffalonian, but in the in the late 1930's, the generosity of Edward Kleinhans, who owned a men's store in Buffalo had the music hall built as a tribute to his wife who loved music, Mary Seaton Kleinhans.

We discussed this fact, making our way to Shelly's for after-program treats.

Shelly lived in a loft, on Elmwood, not far from the music hall. She also owned a beautifully restored Queen Anne off Franklin St. and was on the Buffalo Preservation Board. She rounded out my trinity of *girlfriends*.

Looking at the women I was surrounded by, I truly knew I was a very lucky man. Each woman was in her early 60's, lived through tragedy and happiness, and had unique talents. They were also attractive not only physically, but more so, because they were completely self-less.

Tina, tiny and compact, was a widow who cared for her now grown, grand-daughter, Tia. She taught part-time at ECC and helps refugees settle in the area.

Lenore, who always reminded me of a lovely Snow White with her porcelain skin and dark hair, was raised by a foster family I had found for her and her twin brother Jaime. She's a successful interior decorator, but now runs the Mission with her husband, Harris.

Shelly is an auburn beauty, who attended college with Tina and now helps save historic buildings. She is also a widow. She and Tina double date with decent, honorable men, even though one is a judge, and one is a lawyer.

If I sound sarcastic, it's mainly because I have heard too many horror stories in the confessional of men and women who use their power to mis-carry rules of law in dealing with bankruptcy, foreclosure, and civil suits that have been unfair to the people who have no power. My thoughts were interrupted by Shelly's comment:

"Rob, is it okay with you if we just enjoy some cheesecake tonight with our brandy?"

"Are you really asking?"

"I have an early appointment tomorrow and want to be sharp. We're trying to save a home that may be an E.B. Green. The city wants to level it for a parking lot."

"Who's in charge of making all these renewal decisions?" Lenore asked.

"So far there's a committee headed by responsible people," Tina answered. "But, my grand-daughter says there are people starting to come out for political office from everywhere. She thinks they want to get their finger's in the funding honey pot, the way so many did when our subway to nowhere was being built in the '70's and '80's."

"I remember that debacle," I commented. "Over two hundred forty million dollars evaporated in ten years, and what do we have now? A stretch of line going from downtown to Bailey Ave."

"I hope this transportation thing is resolved, soon," Tina said. "UB North's campus and ECC' South Campus would be connected for the benefit of all, especially me, when I need to get from my home across town."

"Didn't you tell me Tia once dated someone who was running for office, Tina?" I asked.

"Yes. He's the son of a prominent doctor, Justin L. Daniels. Tia told me, the son, Jackson, started out in pre-med, but he soon found himself drawn to politics. He enjoyed debating and realized the potential for making a difference in Buffalo by getting involved through governing."

"Sounds like a winner, Tina." Lenore commented. "What happened? No chemistry for Tia?"

"She really never said, specifically. She wasn't ready to settle down and date for a permanent commitment, yet."

"Isn't Tia building houses, now?" I laughed.

"She is that! I'm going to volunteer, as well, as soon as the weather breaks," Tina laughed in reply.

"What's this now? Why am I always the last to know these things?" Lenore complained.

"You're not out of the loop," I laughed. "We get together to catch up on what's happening."

"Relax, Lenore. Tia's volunteering with *Habitat for Humanity*. I think it helps relieve all the academic stress she's been under trying to get into a PH.D program. She told me working on building things is better for her than going to a gym." Tina explained.

"She's becoming a great woman," Shelly stated. "You must be really proud of her, Tina."

"I don't have to argue that fact." Tina beamed whenever she spoke of her grand-daughter.

"Speaking of arguing," I interrupted, "any news as to whether there's been any progress on making the Central Terminal on Memorial Drive our new train station?"

Shelly was the expert advisor on this. "There're plenty of pros and cons as to whether to build up or tear down, but I hear there's money involved as to where it should be built."

"Developers at war?" I asked.

"Of course. And now politics is getting into the mix. Who's owned by whom, and all that other nonsense." Lenore was stating a basic truth as to why it took so long for Buffalo to break through into the new century.

"Now that you mention it," Tina said, "Tia did mention that Jackson Lloyd once told her that there was interest in his candidacy by a certain political party, with deep pockets."

"We all know who has them in this town," Lenore agreed. "And…we make sure to hit them up hard when we need their financial support for our special fund-raisers."

"Jackson's grandfather was a friend of my father," I unexpectedly revealed.

It had slipped out. Now I had to start explaining without giving too much away. I waited for them to start gabbing. That would get me off the hook, a bit.

"Really? Wasn't that when there was all that mob business around Lewiston and a powerful mob boss?" Tina taught history.

I regretted my blurting out, immediately. I didn't want to reveal Detective Foster and my concern over who might have been involved in certain unsolved murders.

"What? Lenore asked. "Was your father involved with the mob?"

"Does Jackson have a family history of unsavory characters?" Tina asked.

"This is for another time," I managed to keep my voice calm. "Shelly said she needs us to grant her an early evening."

"Alright...for now," Lenore conceded. "But after all the hoopla of your party this week-end subsides, let's re-visit this subject."

"No problem," I lied.

"And, my dear Rob, I'll be by this week with some sketches I've been playing around with for re-doing your rectory wreck."

"I can't wait to see that transformation," Tina and Shelly were in happy mode, forgetting all about the mob thing.

"Thank you, ladies, for a wonderful evening. If you want to stay a bit longer, Lenore, I'll call for a ride."

"Nope. I'm beat too. See you gals soon. We still have to go over the logistics of where to seat people at the big bash this week-end."

"Let them all stand. Then they won't stay that long."

"Thanks, but no thanks for the advice, Rob. Be on your uncivil way. Tina and I are quite capable of organizing people placement," Shelly said.

"Standing burns more calories than sitting," I stated.

"SCAT!!!" they commanded in unison.

# Chapter 12

"You're pretty quiet, Rob," Lenore said as we drove back to the Mission.

"Just tired, dear lady. By the way, have you heard from Nicki and Lowell. Will they be able to get away this weekend to celebrate my antiquity?"

Lenore laughed. "Yes, they'll be here to enjoy your discomfort."

Nicki Kent and her husband, Lowell, live in Canada, tending to Lowell's vineyards at Niagara-on-the Lake. She is my psychic friend. I saved her life from drowning, when she was a teenager and I was just thinking about the priesthood, while a group of us were at Sherkston in Canada. We have been joined in the world of spirit ever since. She is my *special girl.*

"Will Carlos be there, as well?" Carlos is a partner with Shelly's niece, Vanessa in running a fashion design business at the Mission and in Black Rock. C&V Fashions is quite successful in dressing Buffalo ladies in style.

"Yes, Rob. I don't feel like going over the entire guest list with you now, if you don't mind. There's a cast of thousands," she joked.

"I wanted to tell you though before I forget, that the young man you and Tina brought to the Mission to show him there was a better way to live..."

"You mean Leo Jackson?"

"I do. He certainly turned out to be a fine employee of your niece and Carlos. The first time I met him, he looked more like a motorcycle freak. I never thought the world of fashion design would inspire him to turn his life around."

"Yes. Remember how he cursed out Nicki as a witch when he first met her?"

"I do," chuckling at the memory of Nicki's bored face when she told us about it. She was quite used to derision, skepticism, and abuse. I didn't doubt her gift for a minute, and neither did the poor souls she's read for. She is a true communicator with the great beyond.

"Well, Mr. Leo will be at the party as well, and he's bringing a date. It seems that Leo has won a scholarship to the Fashion Institute in New York. Carlos, Vanessa, and I are very proud of him. He's creative, a fast-learner, and destined for a bright future in fashion."

"How's his father doing? Big Al was a mess when Nicki first met him, too."

"He's one of our best carpenters on the construction team, Rob. Those two are a wonderful success stories."

"Happy to hear it. I'm hoping for more, that's for sure."

Lenore dropped me off at the rectory. I wasn't going to play my messages as I was exhausted. But that is one thing I can't seem to resist doing.

The voice of Detective Foster poured out slowly, and deliberately.

"It's just me, Father Rob. I'll be coming to your party this week-end. Just wanted you to know I'm satisfied that nothing more can be done with Judith's case. Everyone's long gone. Your father may have known some of the people involved in all these crimes, but I have no reason to suspect his active participation in any of them. That should set your mind at ease, at least. Let's grab a cup of coffee, though this week. I'd like to pick your mind about another matter."

*Son-of-a-beech*. I can't shake this guy. I didn't know why he was such an annoyance to me. It probably had to do with him bringing up people from my past life I'd like to forget…like my father.

Of course, my sleep was restless, and I dreamed a mess of messes.

It was going to be a relief to untangle their meaning with Nicki. She was the dream whisperer.


## Chapter 13


It was a glorious spring morning for a quick ride over the Border to Niagara-on-the-Lake. I wasn't going to waste any more time trying to solve the unresolved feelings I harbor concerning my father. Nicki can help me untangle my dreams from last night, and maybe I can finally find a way to think of my father without disdain.

The vineyards were leafing a delicate green. I was thrilled that Nicki had found such an appropriate companion in Lowell. She had once asked me to investigate his past, before she could trust his motives for pursuing her. All my *girls,* besides Lenore, have male friends, but have decided to never tie the knot again. I never asked them why marriage was an unpleasant scenario for them. It probably has to do with their independent financial status, and the fact that they already raised their families.

Tina's marriage had been a farce, but Shelly's marriage was ideal. Even though I've heard hundreds of marriage confessions, I've come to understand that each marriage is a unique island, inhabited by a colony of adults and usually children. No one really knows the workings of each marriage. It is almost sacred in its secrecy. I never became jaded with the many stories husbands and wives offered in confession to explain why they wanted out, or had already left, at least emotionally.

The Church I'm a part of doesn't allow divorce, basing its dogma on the Bible's command, "What God has joined together, let no man put asunder." Matthew stated that in marriage the husband and wife are no longer two, but one flesh. I have tried to find a way to rationalize away this decree, that Jesus spoke to the Pharisees about, when they asked Him if Moses allowed divorce. I must face my basic beliefs that God has His own system of checks and balances with little to do with hard and fast rules and regulations. Humans were made with shades of gray. I hope to believe that on judgment day, my life will be reviewed by how much love I showed. Not with the Bible before me, racking up my ability to follow or dismiss the rules and regulations written down in black and white. To me, the Bible is a guide, not a set-in-stone formula for gaining a right to heaven.

And with these meandering thoughts, I saw Nicki waving to me at the gate of the vineyard. She looked like she was enjoying every single minute of her life. Her light brown hair was streaked with sunlight from working outdoors. Her blue eyes matched the color of the sky today.

# Chapter 14

"Welcome, welcome, my dear friend," she said, handing me a crystal glass full of the wine she and Lowell created from plump
Cabernet franc grapes.

"You have a dream you need interpreted?" she joked. "I haven't seen you in almost a year, and now I'm going to have the privilege of seeing you twice in one week?"

"My dear Nicki, you are prescient."

The vineyard was alive with new growth. Besides the acres of staked grape vines, there was a huge bed of tulips, daffodils, hyacinths, and lilac bushes. A floral palette of pastels. These would be replaced by summer plants and flowers in June. There were benches surrounding the larger trees, for us mere mortals to sit and enjoy the beauty of a bountiful land.

"Well, then. Let's sit under this great spreading oak and begin the process. We can chat afterwards. I see you have some deep wound that needs to be lanced."

"Thanks, Nicki. I want to settle something once and for all. Someone recently managed to dredge up my past. I thought certain feelings had been buried. Zombies are real. Those feelings are coming back to haunt me and could eat me alive."

"Wow. Let's get to it then. Sit here. Relax. Close your eyes and let your dream spill out in the open."

Taking a deep breath, I closed my eyes and focused on the dreams from last night.

"I was about 16 years old, sitting on the beach at our summer home in Canada. I felt peaceful. My father comes rushing down the beach stairs with a sheet of paper in his hand. His face is red with fury.
He throws the paper at me, which is as heavy as a rock.

He says, 'We'll see about this!' And storms off.

I pick up the paper, rubbing my forehead where the paper hit and see blood on my fingers. The blood increases and starts flowing down covering the paper so I cannot read what may be on it. I start crying uncontrollably. My mother calls from the house telling me lunch is ready and to stop blubbering. I get up, but the paper is now balled up and has grown into a huge granite boulder. I wake up."

"Any other dreams last night?" Nicki asked, softly. "Keep your eyes closed."

I do as she asks, and a dream appears, that I was not even aware of dreaming last night. It's as if I'm in a hypnotic state, and my unconscious is releasing important information. I begin to speak, relating what I am seeing through a semi-conscious lens My surroundings are blocked out. My dream state is real.

*"I'm in my late teens, passing by my father's Study. He's smoking a cigar as are his friends. He tells me to come in and meet them. I step inside, am given a Scotch and a cigar. Looking around I see five other men wearing three-piece suits. One of them is my father's friend, now a judge, Jason Lloyd Daniels. The cigar smoke is choking me. I can barely make out the men's faces until the smoke clears. Their features have turned into wolves, swine, and snakes. I'm trying to leave, but my father grabs ahold of my arm and tells the others that I'm thinking of the priesthood." Their laughter finally allows me to wake up."*

Nicki puts her arm around my shoulder.

"Lots of unresolved pain, right Rob?"

"I thought it had been," I sighed. Then this detective came to see me about an unsolved murder and all these issues with my father began re-surfacing."

"A detective?"

"It's a long story for another time. I have another appointment to attend to this afternoon. Does anything about my dreams jump out at you for now?"

"We've had discussions about your relationship with your father before, Rob. You forgave him on his deathbed, if I recall."

"As a priest, but not as a son, apparently."

"Hmmm. I see."

"Do you?" I asked, remembering how my father confessed to me he was hard on me because he wanted me to be successful and follow his lead. How he had hated the idea of me becoming a priest.

"Your father never beat you, but he emotionally hurt you by bullying you into doing his bidding. Was becoming a priest your way of bullying him?"

"I thought it was. But after I was ordered by the judge to choose the military or the priesthood in place of jail for stealing that car, I grew to love the spiritual side of life."

"This acceptance of your new life away from material aspirations angered your father?"

"Infuriated him. He thought my hedonistic lifestyle would make me hate the Sem and I would come crawling back to him, begging for a place in his Company."

"Fathers and sons make complicated relationships. Do you know that some fathers are jealous of their own son's happiness at times?"

"Yes. It's not something easy to own up to."

"I'm sure you've heard much anguish in the confessional, in regard to how sons feel unworthy in deserving their father's love and respect. And…how some fathers are ashamed they resent their own sons' accomplishments."

"Yes. But I don't know what that bloody paper means, or the cigar smoke. Besides, my father eventually forgave my life choice. He left me with quite a fortune."

"I believe Rob, the unresolved feelings of resentment have more to do this time with your mother, not your father."

"Really?" I was taken by surprise.

"The second dream shows that even though you rejected your father and his friends' way of life, he eventually accepted your choice and was even able to joke about it."

"I believe the paper your father threw at you has deeper meaning, and the part about its meaning being hidden by blood, then turning into a huge granite rock may mean you still have a stone to over-turn, especially in relation to your mother who you believe didn't seem to care that you were deeply hurt by your father."

That was a huge, eye-opening analysis. "It's true my mother never told my father to lay off me. She was really quite docile, never questioning my father. I don't think she was afraid of him. It was more of…I don't know? Something more like loyalty."

"Have you ever seen your birth certificate, Rob?"

"Just copies of it."

"See if you can dig up a copy of the original. A feeling has prompted me to ask about it. You may be able to find out what is being hidden from you."

"You're kidding, right?"

"Don't be too astonished. Many people live their entire lives not knowing their true origins."

"Do you think my dreams are urging me to find mine?"

"Let me know if I'm right about this. Come up to the house, now for some tea and tidbits."

"I truly wish I could, but I have an hour to get back to Buffalo. I sincerely hope we get together more than we have, Nicki. Let's plan something after the big bash this week-end."

She heartily agreed and gave me a much-needed hug.


## Chapter 15


I was quite agitated driving back, and decided to take the longer route along the river to the Peace Bridge. I needed the ions of the Falls I would be passing to replenish my spirit. I needed to think about and digest the information about my mother and my original birth certificate.

It was a good time for me to pray for guidance in helping me find the meaning of a piece of paper, capable of hitting me squarely in the head.

I had some quality time to think on my drive back from Canada. The road home on the Canadian side is scenic, full of tree-lined lanes and beautiful houses.

The face of one poor woman, floated up to my consciousness. I work, spiritually, with Hospice. Many times, people cannot get to confession, so I come to them. This particular day, I re-called leaving the Hospice center, when a thin voice called out from one of the rooms.

"Please come in here. Come in here. Yes, you, in the black suit."

I entered the room to find a thin, frail woman, lying in bed, hands folded across her chest.

"I'm not Catholic. I just wanna know what all this confession thing is about. Why are you sneaking around to everyone, listening to them whine about their lives?"

"Are you upset that I give these people comfort, Ma'am?"

"I'm not your *Ma'am* young man." At that time, I must have been in my 50's.

"Sorry. How might I address you?"

She opened her watery blue eyes and said, "My name is Florence. Florence Miller."

"How do you do Florence Miller." My respectful tone seemed to calm her. She visibly relaxed and asked me to hand her one of the hard candies on her bed stand.

I began to visit her every week. The nurses told me she should have already died. There was no physical reason for her to still be alive. She was suffering from congestive heart failure, had COPD, breast cancer, and other ailments. She entered Hospice when she was 90 years old. She was about to celebrate her 93rd birthday!

"We don't know what's making her stay alive," one of the nurses told me. "I know God works in mysterious ways, but this one is truly a mystery. With the amount of morphine we're giving her, and the body weight she's lost, I think her will to live is more powerful than death's grasp."

This situation was a mystery. I found out on my fourth visit to Florence, the reason for her staunch refusal to let go.

"To tell you the truth, Robert, I'm afraid. I'm afraid when I die, all the people I hurt will be there to torture me."

"Tell me about it, Florence." I did not minimize her fear. It was apparent that it was strong enough to defy death itself.

"I'm stubborn, Robert. Just my nature. My mother raised me and my sis to be strong women. She had to raise us by herself after my father died when we were just young girls. She taught us how to survive, and was angry that my father was a weak man who hanged himself to escape life."

I understood how her childhood made her stingy with others. "You weren't going to be a victim, were you, Florence?"

"Damn right. I was going to be Bette Davis. Screw Julie Andrews."

"Great analogy," I smiled.

"Anyway, I married my husband for the security of having my own home. Believe it or not, I was very cute back then. So, Rodney fell for me. I found out when we were engaged that he had fathered a son before meeting me, when he had just returned from the Service, before he moved back to Buffalo. The kid was three when his mother came visiting my Rodney in order to work something out. I was scared to death that all the security I wanted would vanish, and Rodney would choose her and the kid over me. I was already in my late 20's. No one else was in the picture to take care of me."

"Did Rodney explain to you that this past life of his wouldn't break your relationship with him?"

"No. He felt torn, and I cried my eyes out. So, he chose to marry me out of pity instead of claiming his son and marrying his mother."

She was silent for a bit. Then came the confession.

"I forbade him to pay any child support to his son's mother. I told him he would never be allowed to have a relationship with them."

"And he obeyed?"

She let out a great sigh of release

"Found out he sneaked over from Rochester, where we had lived, after we were married, to Buffalo, in order to see them once in a while and gave them money."

"Was that so bad?"

"No. Now I see that. Back then I was furious. To punish him, we slept in separate rooms. To punish me, he became a bitter, penny-pinching spouse."

"You never had children of your own?"

"No. I had a few cats. He had golf and hunting buddies. If I hadn't been so stubborn and jealous, our life might have been a lot happier for all of us."

I held her frail hand. "Florence, your life has been your punishment. There is going to be a happy ending when you leave your poor body and allow your spirit to fly to heaven. No one is allowed in heaven who holds grudges or seeks revenge. Hate is banned from the after-life."

"Are you sure?" she squeezed my hand as much as she could.

"I am certain of this," I stated firmly, placing my other hand on her forehead, smoothing out her worried lines. I also asked her permission to bestow a blessing.

She nodded and sighed a great sigh of relief.

The next morning Hospice called to tell me Florence Miller had entered into eternal life, peacefully.

# Chapter 16

Thankfully, the Peace Bridge traffic was not that bad. Border Patrol asked me the usual questions and I was allowed to cross over to the USA without much of a problem. I was a white male after all. There are certain privileges granted to us *special creations*. Of course, this galls me, but I am a helpless pawn in this particular *Game of Thrones.*

If my luck held out, I would be able to keep my afternoon appointment with Jackson Daniels.

Jackson has an office in City Hall as a comptroller. He is one of the watch dogs making sure tax payers' money was being used wisely and well. I wanted to ask his if his interest in the Mission was because of some illegal activity suspected there.

On my way to his office, I stopped by the Records Office and filled out a form for my birth certificate, stating I would be back in a half hour to retrieve it.

City Hall offices were unimpressive, though they often were stepping stones to higher, much better- appointed offices in Albany. My own rectory office was much more well-appointed than the Comptroller's, and that's saying a lot.

"Glad to finally meet you, Father Sullivan." Jackson Daniels was an amiable young man in his early 30's, very clean-cut and handsome. He would do well earning the trust of his constituents if he was truly interested in running for office.

"Happy you were able to fit me in your schedule at such short notice, Mr. Daniels."

"No problem. I was going to call you for an appointment soon, myself, Father. Detective Foster told you of my interest in the Mission?"

"Yes. That's why I'm here. Can you tell me what this is all about?"

"First, I want you to know, I know my grandfather and your father were friends. I know my grandfather was not always a scandal-free lawyer. He represented many shady characters. I don't believe your father was ever involved in the lives or situations my family's had to back away from."

"I appreciate your being honest about this, Mr. Daniels. My father and I were estranged until he was near death. I didn't know much about my father's business associates, and neither did my sister."

"She was killed in a motorcycle accident, my father told me. Her boyfriend was an uncle of mine."

"This is I did not know," I replied, shocked that the rebellious young man my sister was involved with was a relation of the Daniels' family. So many new connections to the Daniels I was just learning about. Jackson knew more about my family than I did.

"He was considered one of our numerous black sheep. He wanted no part of the family business and was the rebel, causing my father and our relatives embarrassing explanations and many pay-offs to the legal community."

"This is all news to me," I was stunned. "I think I may have already been studying for the priesthood. My mother was devastated by this tragedy, naturally, but my father was angry that his daughter's own rebellious behavior caused his family's private life to be so publicly exposed as not perfect."

It always amazed me how scandal was superficial fear of appearing less than better than the next family. Everyone has skeletons. Real people, that is; Not TV projections.

"Our families have much in common when it comes to hiding its share of scandals, Father. But, the reason I was investigating the Mission has to do with the opioid epidemic in our community. You may already be aware that I'm interested in running for State Assembly. I wanted to make sure that the refugees housed at the Mission weren't involved in helping distribute any pills they might be receiving from their doctors to make money on the side."

This was another shocking revelation. "I hope your investigation turned up nothing in that regard."

"So far. I want to use this drug issue as part of my platform. Too many of our citizens have had their families destroyed by this epidemic."

"The first place you look for the source of these pills is where the most vulnerable are housed?"

"I think of them as the most desperate, so forgive me, Father."

"I'm beginning to understand how you're going to try to persuade potential voters that they should fear our new immigrants and refugees and that you are the one to go to Albany to allay those fears."

"That's a bit harsh, Father, but this is the right time to use the public's fear as an opportunity to gain their votes."

"Thank you for being so starkly honest, Mr. Daniels. At least you're not a hypocrite. I wish you well, but I hope you know that now that you've revealed your political plans, I'm going to do everything I can to thwart your political ambitions."

"I was hoping the opposite, Father. I know you have close ties with the wife and sister-in-law of one of our State Senators" He was referring to Shelly's sister, who was married to the Senator.

"I know many connected people, Mr. Daniels. That's why I feel confident I can deter you from using the most vulnerable as stepping stones to a political future."

"Thank you, Father Sullivan, for being so honest with me. But, I'm not moved by your threats. Your generation is dying out. Voters, today, want to rid Albany of all the corruption your generation has helped to thrive. I'm going to be able to show them how Buffalo and Albany can rid itself of all the hand-outs and irresponsible fiscal spending on programs that have done nothing to help our citizens."

"I see, Mr. Daniels. So instead of being corrupt as your grandfather was in illegal activities with politicians and the mob, you're going to clean your family's legacy by using the poor as scapegoats for all the problems of the State."

"It's time everyone takes personal responsibility for their own happiness, Father. We can't take care of the world anymore. People are ready to take action to rid themselves of these burdens and focus on infrastructure and modern technical jobs. It's a new kind of revolution, Father. Times are changing at warp speed. These drugs are hurting progress."

"I see. Drugs have started to hurt the white upper middle class, so now they're bad. When the ghetto was fighting crack and cocaine, there wasn't much of a public outcry. But now statistics show that the people hooked on heroin are those hooked first on pain drugs. It's going to be a powerful campaign issue for you, Mr. Daniels. Please stop harassing the residents at the Mission, though. They're going through enough without having to worry about imaginary issues dreamed up to help you get elected."

"This has been an interesting meeting, Father Sullivan. I need to meet with other constituents. Know that my investigation at the Mission is over for now. I'm going to have to focus on irresponsible doctors, now, who by the way, are mostly immigrants, using their prescription orders to help make an affluent living off the pain of paying patients."

"Interesting, to say the least, Mr. Daniels. I'll be watching your campaign efforts closely. I, too must be going. I too have other constituents to meet with. They also need a voice. A more sympathetic one, I might add."

## Chapter 17

I almost forgot to retrieve my birth certificate on my way out. It was disturbing to think positively of this young man who was so willing to throw so many helpless people under the bus for his own ambitions. Was this really that different from the "hits" used by organized crime syndicates? It really does seem that politics is a legal name for today's organized crime full of pay-offs, bribery, and corruption.

My thoughts were interrupted by the clerk in the records office stating that I had no birth certificate on file.

"Are you sure you were born in Buffalo?"

"I thought I was. But in my family, we never asked too many questions," I joked.

"This often happens when people were born in Niagara Falls," she said. "Do you want me to call over and save you a trip?"

"Can you do that?"

"I will, for you, Father Sullivan. You helped my family out of jams, many times."

"Are you a parishioner?"

"I am but at the church on Delaware, where you used to be assigned. Also, my mother was in Hospice at Kenmore Mercy. You gave her much comfort."

It pays, to show kindness and compassion, I was thinking, when the clerk retuned to inform me that yes indeed, my records were at the Niagara Falls City Hall.

I needed to calm down before leaving for home. I took an elevator to the stairs on the 25th floor of City Hall, leading to the Observation Deck. This little detour helped me rise above the political mess I had just witnessed with Daniels. The beautiful city looked peaceful in the afternoon sun. Its streets radiated like the spokes of a wheel, designed to hinder an attack. Poor Buffalo was burned to the ground more than 200 years ago in 1813, in retaliation by the British for Americans burning down Niagara-on-the-Lake and Toronto, then named York. History is so full of violence, I am thankful to be living in this century in America, a land of peace and prosperity, at least, so far.

Driving back to the Mission, I was exhausted by all the shocking events of this day. I would attempt a visit to Niagara Falls tomorrow.

I was in desperate need of a nap. Thank you, Lord, for Tina's doggie bag waiting for me to warm up its left-overs from the other night. I was whipped, determined to not let my mind interrupt my need for a dreamless sleep.

# Chapter 18

The next morning, after Mass, I headed out for Niagara Falls. Lenore never asked why I needed to borrow her car. She knew I never took it out for a mere joy ride.

I did enjoy the drive to Niagara Falls. It's fallen on hard times since Mayor E. Dent Lackey destroyed its unique ambiance by getting rid of all the small boutiques that used to line Falls Street to create the worthless Rainbow Mall, in the name of Urban Renewal. Hopefully, new life will also revive its down-trodden neighborhoods. The Canadian side at Clifton Hill was and is much more vibrant, but now, not as accessible, thanks to homeland security protecting us from terrorists.

My birth certificate was waiting for me. I retrieved it, deciding to have a quick lunch at the Culinary Institute on Falls Street. This was one place that is a sign of successful re-building, but even it has recently seen signs of corruption in regard to its funding. When in heaven's name will we ever get over our love affair with the golden calf?

My appetite for a lobster roll and Manhattan clam chowder was interrupted by my buzzing cell. I wasn't going to answer, but it was that gnat of a detective, and I was getting angry about his intrusion into my personal time.

"What now, Detective?"

"I sense hostility, Father." He was actually laughing. "I see you're at *Savor* and was hoping you'd allow me to stop by. I have some interesting information I'd like to share with you."

"How do you know where I am? Are you stalking me, again?"

"Don't you know if you don't turn off your location app, anyone can find out where you are at any given time?"

"Thanks for that important info. Where are you now, by the way? Hiding behind some bush outside the restaurant?"

He was laughing loudly now. "I'm no Pink Panther, Father, but I am just up the block. I was visiting the manager of the Casino."

"As long as you don't ruin my entire lunch. I'm here, so you might as well slither down."

"Not nice, Father Sullivan. But, I think you'll see it'll be worth it to you to hear what I have to say about Mr. Daniels."

I really could have cared less at this moment; but since I still had a sour taste in my mouth after my visit with Daniels, I was a bit interested in what Detective Foster had to say.

Waiting for the detective to appear, I took the copy of my birth certificate from its envelope. I glanced at the names on it, and suddenly felt myself turning inside out. There was no father listed! The mother's name was Silvia Rose Daniels. The date of birth was different from the date my birthday was celebrated by my family. This had to be a mistake! Whose birth certificate was this? My name was Robert James Sullivan as the child born to Silvia Rose Daniels?

"Is something wrong, Father Sullivan?"

Detective Foster was seating himself across from me, alarmed by my sudden shocked appearance.

"Perfect timing, Detective. It now looks like I'm in dire need of an investigator, myself."

I handed him the copy of my birth certificate. He did not look surprised.

"It's taken you all these years to uncover one of your family's deepest secrets," he said gently. "Your birth mother was a daughter of your father's friend and business associate, Jason Lloyd Daniels. Your father and mother adopted you as a favor to the Daniels' family. It seems your father's business needed more investment capital and he made a deal with Daniels to spare his family scandal. Your birth mother died in a car accident, shortly after your birth."

I was shocked into silence, staring at the detective, as if waiting for a video in further explanation.

"Looking into the Daniels family as much as I have, in relation to my step-sister, Judith's death, I found information on the daughter who was killed in an auto accident. I looked up her medical records, and found she had recently given birth to a child. She wasn't married, so I dug deeper, and found that there was an adoption record for a male child, filed by your father and mother, listing Robert James Sullivan as the adopted child."

"There's no one alive in my family to corroborate this story, Detective. I'm stunned by this."

"Of course. Your mother insisted on filling in your adopted name on your original birth certificate, as she felt that it solidified your existence on the planet, and allowed for you to be baptized in the Church. Otherwise, there would have been no official record of your birth. You would have been *Baby X.*"

"That's why my name is given on my Baptismal Certificate and copies of my Birth Certificate have my mother's name listed as Mary Louise Sullivan, instead of my birth mother, Silvia Rose Daniels."

"You weren't the only child whose birth certificate was doctored like yours. Many family's hid illegitimate births this way when having such a child was a deep scandal. This doesn't happen today, of course. There is no stigma attached to single mothers giving birth, even in the best of families."

"I'm still in shock, though, Detective. This means that the Daniels family and myself are related by blood! It also means I am really older by at least a month!"

"You've done well through the years, though, Father. Despite all the dysfunction of your family, you've helped a great many people."

Detective Foster's compliment was genuine. I felt myself becoming more in touch with reality.

"Does Jackson know I'm related to his family? Does his father?"

"That's why I'm here, Father. Justin Daniels, Jackson's father is your uncle. He's a retired MD, still seeing his older patients at his home on Delaware. You should pay him a visit to learn more, if possible. See how much he knows about his sister's life."

"My God, Detective. If I'm 75, he must be..."

"90, to be exact. He had a second wife, when he was 60."

"What happened to his first wife?"

"You'll have to ask Dr. Daniels. I haven't had time to look up her death certificate."

"It's beginning to make more sense now. My father wanted me to inherit his wealth, not the Church, but he also didn't want the Daniels family laying claim to his money by proving that I was really a Daniels and not a Sullivan. Or, maybe my father knew who my biological father was and didn't want his money going to that family either."

"That's what I'm thinking, too. I wonder why your father didn't confess the whole mess to you before he died?"

"That's a mystery. My mother passed away before my father, but she never breathed a word to me, either."

"Your father must have sworn her to secrecy for some reason. But, now I'm also wondering if Jackson knows you two are related and somehow thinks he can get his hands on your considerable estate after you pass on."

"Guess I'll have to do some investigating, myself, Detective."

"You can call me *Martin*, Father Sullivan. I'm not trying to trick you or blame you or find you guilty of anything."

"Thanks, Martin. I'm sorry if I've been less than cordial. Old wounds, you know. Didn't think I'd have to open up scars from my youth at this stage of the game."

"I realize this must all be shocking, Father Sullivan."

"Please. You should call me *Rob*. I think we have too much in common to be so formal any longer."

"Thank you. We'll get to the bottom of all this, Rob. We're almost there now. I think we only have to find out if Jackson Daniels is playing you to cash in on your inheritance, or if he really is investigating the Mission to find out if it's a drug store for selling illegal opioids."

Martin gave me Jackson's father's address. I would pay him a visit this afternoon right before I was to meet my girls for a late supper at one of my favorite Asian noodle shops.

# Chapter 19

Doctor Daniels house was easy to find on Delaware Ave. Parking was not. I was able to squeeze into a spot a few houses down. Luckily my parallel parking skills were still efficient.

The small sign under the massive oak door knocker read *Justin L. Daniels, MD.;Hours by Appointment.*

I tried the door, and it opened, easily. There was an entrance hall, and to the left was a waiting room, where three persons were seated, waiting to see their doctor. I hadn't been in one of these types of waiting rooms since I was a young man, when private MDs held office hours in their personal homes. Dark wainscot paneling. Leather chairs along the walls. Persian rug resting on oak flooring. Oil paintings of bucolic scenes. Reading lamps, dimly lit to display magazines such as *Time, National Geographic*, and *Buffalo Spree.* A nurse opened a door and called a Mr. Adams into the inner office. I asked her if I would be able to see the doctor today, even if I didn't have a formal appointment.

She took note of my Roman collar and wrote down my name.

"It will be about an hour, Father, if you don't mind waiting." She sounded pleasant enough and was quite young and attractive.

I said I would be happy to wait.

Taking a seat, I reached for a *National Geographic,* while surreptitiously studying the other patients. There was one man and two women, all elderly, my age or older. I was no longer nonplussed admitting that I was now an *elderly person,* although I wouldn't admit to it till I had turned 70.

No one spoke to each other, though I could feel their eyes studying me.

The young nurse called me in after 45 minutes, I was the last patient. It was 3:30 PM.

I was ushered into an examining room, to await the doctor. I almost fainted when Dr. Daniels entered. It was like looking at myself in a mirror. The resemblance was astonishing. He was tall, like me, had my blue eyes, and his thick white hair was combed back off his forehead like mine. He was older, I knew, but it seems as if people between 80 and 90 are in an age-holding pattern.

"Good afternoon, Father Sullivan. I'm quite surprised it's taken this long for our paths to cross." Smiling, it became clear that Dr. Daniels knew exactly who I was.

"It appears you know who I am, Dr. Daniels." I was trying to keep my voice calm. I felt very agitated, however.

"Have a seat and let's get this all out in the open. It's really no big deal."

"To me it is, Dr. Daniels." I was now feeling annoyed.

"Please, call me *Justin*."

"At least you didn't ask to be called *Uncle Justin*." I smiled crookedly. He responded with a hearty laugh. The ice was broken. I started laughing, myself.

"This is ridiculous, isn't it, Father Sullivan?"

"How do you mean, Justin? And please call me *Rob*."

"I mean the situation our families put us in because they were so afraid of scandal back in the '40's and '50's, when there was so much social upheaval beginning. You'd think they would have come clean before everyone passed away."

"I would have been none the wiser, Justin, but for the fact that I recently discovered my original birth certificate."

"Really?"

"Your sister was my birth mother?"

"Again. I must explain, I wasn't in on the secret when I was young. I only knew that my sister was sent away on a retreat to Italy, the Vatican, no less. When she returned, she was involved in an automobile accident which took her life."

"Then when did you find out the truth?"

"One of my father's old friends came to me about a medical issue. I helped him control his chronic pain. It slipped out that he was sorry about my sister's having an unhappy life because she couldn't marry the man she had loved. I pretended I knew what he was talking about. He spilled the beans, thinking I knew all about my sister being involved with one of the sons of a mob leader from Lewiston.

*Too bad your father was so against your poor sister being happy even if it meant having a life controlled by the Magaddino family.*

I agreed with him, even though this was all news to me, at the time. My father was already dead, so I couldn't ask him about this. My mother was the only one I could ask, though she was already suffering from dementia in a Nursing Home. I decided to try and find out what I could from her, anyway."

"How long ago was this?"

"I was in my 40's, so it was about 50 years ago."

"Were you able to find out anything from your mother?"

I was hoping his response wouldn't lead to more complications. Why did I feel a sense of dread overcoming me. It had started out to be such a pleasant day. Was there still time for me to book a flight to Pago-Pago, or somewhere else, so I wouldn't be here, right in the middle of Scandal Soup?

Detective Foster burst my wishing bubble.

"Enough to know that my sister did have a baby that was given up for adoption. At the time, I thought it was in Italy. My mother was very confused when I asked about my sister, Silvia's baby. She may not have even have known about it all, herself. My father never talked much about anything concerning his business friends and clients. She said Silvia kept crying when she returned from Italy and wanted to see her baby. My mother started crying saying Silvia began drinking too much and that's when she drove her car into a tree."

"I'm sorry, Justin. Our families seem to have been messed up quite a bit. It's amazing we both came out, fairly unscathed."

"I did some investigating on my own, and found the original birth certificate and learned that my family and the Magaddinos had a big falling out. People were killed, fighting over turf, and mistrust. My father was murdered because he was seen as a stoolie, I think. I don't know if the Magaddinos even knew that one of their family members was the father of my sister's baby. That's one of the reasons I didn't want to reveal what I had found out. To keep you safe, I shut my mouth. Of course, I learned what I could about you and how you were raised. When I found out you were studying for the priesthood, I decided to let sleeping dogs lie. There was no reason to disrupt your life with re-opening the scandals my family, and most likely yours, were involved with."

"What happened to the Magaddino family?"

"They were ousted from power and left with a small faction to control till Stefano Magaddino died in 1974."

"I was born in 1942. Do you have any idea who my birth father was?"

"Sorry, Rob. That I could not discover. My sister and I were sheltered from my father's private life and associates. However, we both had friends who were as much in the dark as to what our fathers did as we were. We were all brought up in a time when children were seen but not heard. The Magaddinos legitimate business was in running a Funeral Home."

"How convenient," I joked.

"They also ran legitimate businesses in the service industry, providing linens to hotels, and taxi-cabs. The children of these mobsters had no idea that they were tied to La Cosa Nostra. When my sister fell in love with a young guy from one of these families, my father panicked and realized he didn't want family ties to unite with his business ties. Being Catholic, he also didn't want his daughter to suffer through an abortion. Plus, it wasn't legal and he didn't want to take a chance of it being publicized and attract the attention of the vindictive family known for its revenge activities."

"Does your son know any of this and my connection to your family?"

"Jackson is trying to get involved with politics. I couldn't find any other evidence to explain who your father was and who my sister was involved with. I think it best that he believes what the truth is as you know it. You're Father Robert Sullivan, son of the deceased Sullivans, who left a substantial estate to you and which you are using to do the best possible good."

"It seems that you're a good man, Justin, interested in helping people through your medical practice. I have to agree with you, though, that there's not much benefit in dredging up the past. My birth father is probably long deceased, and I have no progeny to protect from scandal. I've lived and am living a rewarding life so...."

"If you ever want to stop by for a chat, Rob, feel free. I don't leave the house much these days. Everything I need is right here. My lovely young nurse efficiently takes good care of me and my patients. It's been a pleasure meeting you in person. In case you haven't noticed, we do have a strong family resemblance. You look like I did in my 70's."

"Oh, I've noticed," I laughed. Hopefully I can look as good as you in twenty years, and still be as active."

"Being with my patients, keeps me going, Rob. I take care of their bodies; you take care of their souls."

"Thank you for seeing me, Justin. You can count on me dropping in now and again for a chat and a cup of tea."

"Looking forward to it, my friend, new and old."


I was content and pleased that I had taken a chance in meeting up with Dr. Daniels. It brought me the information I was needing to fill in the blanks Detective Foster... Martin, had left for me to fill in.

Now to meet with my girls and act as if I am still the same person they have always known. I didn't feel any different, but I will definitely be more aware of what Jackson Daniels is up to on his way to higher political office.

# Chapter 20

I love Asian noodles; be they Korean, Vietnamese, Chinese, or Japanese. I also love sharing my meals with *my girls.*

Seated at a round table at Saigon Bangkok, I felt intense love for these lovely women, no longer young in body, but timelessly beautiful in spirit.

"This dinner is on me ladies. I feel generous as well as extremely hungry this evening."

"You always pick up the tab, Rob." Lenore commented.

"And you're always famished," Tina added.

"But you're in an extremely good mood tonight," Shelly noticed.

"I am, aren't I? I feel like a new man. Must be Spring and the lovely company tonight."

"Good to see you not your usual grumpy self," Tina laughed. "You know I'm kidding. I have rarely seen you in a bad mood, ever."

"Being a guest of honor at a party can put me in a foul mood, as you've probably noticed. But since we agreed it's going to be more like a fund-raiser, I can deal with it."

"Your modesty is almost pride-full," Tina admonished. "Plus, it makes us uncomfortable when you appear holier than us. Just because we love you, doesn't mean we can't point out your flaws."

"Thank God, Tina. I wouldn't ever presume to be perfect. It's my imperfections that allow us to get along so well together."

It felt so good to laugh. There was no better tonic.

I had decided not to reveal my newly discovered family to these lovely ladies. What good would this accomplish? I still needed to digest all this astonishing information, privately. Still, I felt elated. The mystery as to why my father and I had so many disagreements was revealed. It hadn't been about me at all. It was about my father having had to raise me, not by choice, but by being forced to because of a loan he had received to bolster up a failing business. My father didn't ever want to be beholden to anyone. Apparently, every time he looked at me, he was seeing a reminder of his personal failing as a business man. He had needed to be bailed out. My mother was also apparently not in on the deal. She may even have believed that I was the result of a tryst between my father, her husband, and some other woman. This would explain her hands-off approach to me. It also explained my birth certificate. Someone, other than my parents must have doctored it. My father could have easily paid off someone to add his surname to mine, in order to protect the family assets from being claimed by the Daniels family.

"Except when we sprang on him our plans for celebrating his life with a big party," Shelly said, interrupting my thoughts.

"Don't remind me," I answered. "I might just become sullen, thinking about it all."

"Fine," Lenore said. "What else is new with you?"

"Earth to Rob…Did you hear what I just asked?" Lenore had interrupted my intense musings.

"Sorry, Lenore. A senior moment of mental wandering."

"Please, Rob," Shelly said. "There's no way you're entering your dotage yet. We need all your wise faculties to help us through our declining years."

"If you girls are in decline, I feel sorry for Western Civilization." I was not really joking. "If it wasn't for you and all your fair sex we might all still be cave-dwellers. I can't even begin to enumerate all the progress we've made through the ages because of the efforts of women, behind the scenes. I know women are still being put aside as mere appendages from men, because of Adam's rib story, but you all are more like the backbone of everything that's been accomplished in life."

"Wow!!! I'm impressed by this vote of confidence coming from a man wo grew up during the '50's." Tina's comment was not meant to be sexist. Her husband had made full use of his masculine wiles to use and abuse women. As a highly-respected professor, he used his status to attract women who were flattered by his attention, then succumbed to his sexual advances. He was not the first man to use his position to manipulate women. Hopefully, this type of abuse was slowly but surely declining, thanks to women standing up and voicing their experiences with this type of sexual aggression.

"I asked you if it was okay with you if I came by Thursday or Friday morning with some preliminary sketches for your study re-do."

"Lenore, you don't even have to show me your sketches. I know you'll do a great job, as usual."

"Then, we'll all come by Rob. We can't wait to see the before and after," Shelly was excited by my agreeing to Lenore's office re-decorating efforts. "I was ready to suggest your office being placed on the protected Buffalo structures for preservation status."

The ladies smiled, giggling like the young girls they have always been in spirit. I was happy they were in my life. We've been friends for over 40 years.

"Is everything all set, then, for this Saturday's fiasco?" I asked.

"That's not nice, Rob," Tina complained. "Many people you've helped want this opportunity to thank you for your service. Don't deny them the pleasure of personally honoring you."

"When you put it that way, Tina, it makes me even less enthusiastic about this bash. I don't want to be honored, or thanked, or even noticed. My job is to help people with their moral dilemmas. More often than not, they've solved their own quandaries and predicaments by talking about them with me. I am the most reasonably priced therapist there is. I'm free."

"You just have to suck it up, Rob." Shelly was adamant. "We want to have this public party, and we've catered to your every wish from hot dogs to polka bands. If you must, think of all this as just a gigantic get-together. At least, from my point of view, it will give people a chance to see the majesty of the Central Terminal, and realize why we need to preserve it."

"So be it, then, Shelly. I can look at this as a benefit to preserve that magnificent building and a chance for Lenore to expand her revitalization of the east side of Buffalo, emanating from the Mission's epi-center."

They all laughed in relief at arriving at a compromise. I was able to come to terms with their party plans. They were happy, even though I pretended to be.

Truth be told, I was afraid of running into people who confessed the most heinous of acts to me, and who I was not able to guide back onto the correct moral path.

# Chapter 21

On my way back to the rectory, I stopped by the church I loved and felt the most at home in. I wanted to review all the confessions I considered failures on my part, and ask our Lord to forgive me for my failings. There were a few persons I was unable to give comfort to or absolution. They would have to remain in hell here on earth with their consciences, until they could bear it no longer and change their ways. Of course, I realized that by even attempting to confess, they at least admitted to having consciences. The people who could sin without regret or remorse were hopeless in their eternal condemnation. That, or they were either morally bankrupt or mentally ill.

One nurse had confessed she regularly confiscated pain pills from the doctor she worked for to support her own habit and that of her boyfriend.

*"I can't stop, Father, because we're addicted, and I can't afford to lose my job."*

I hadn't realized the opioid epidemic was so horribly prevalent at the time, so I merely told her to go into rehab or even change jobs. I wondered, later, if she was one of the unfortunate souls found dead in her car from over-dosing, with the needle still in her arm.

Another contrite teenager confessed he had struck his grandmother because she had refused to give him money.

*"I just got so angry because I knew she was loaded and could afford to throw a few bucks my way."*

*"Do you work to earn money for yourself?"*

*"I work in a restaurant, but it costs plenty to live these days. The girl I live with wants me to chip in more and now we're going to have a baby, as if we can afford that."*

*"So, what's your plan?"* I asked as non-judgmentally as I could.

*"I'm going to ask my grandmother if we could move in with her. That way she can see and take care of her grandchild, and we won't have to worry so much 'bout making ends meet."*

*"Do you think you could get a better job?"*

*"I didn't finish high school. There aren't any good paying jobs out there. Do you want me to sell drugs?"*

*"I hope you can control your temper more, or soon you'll be physically abusing not only your grandmother, but also your girlfriend, and even your own child. Can you get your GED?"*

*"You're making things too complicated. I just wanna be forgiven for hitting my grandma. Don't lecture me on how I should live the rest of my life."*

He was getting himself worked up, as he slammed out of the confessional.

One of the worst confessions I had to listen to was from a man who hated his wife so much, he was planning on a way to get rid of her, permanently.

*"She tricked me into marrying her fifteen years ago, by pretending she was pregnant. We haven't had relations since, but she knows how to cash my paycheck. She knows how to yell at me, criticize me, make me clean the house. I hate her, Father. I want to pay someone to get rid of her for me."*

*"Have you been to counseling?"*

*"She laughs at the idea and says I'm the one causing all the problems"*

*"Have you thought about divorce?"*

*"I thought the Catholic Church is against it."*

"It is, but there are ways around the taboo. Of course, money was involved.

*"There are annulments allowed when one party can prove collusion at the onset, like your wife did to trick you into marrying her."*

*"I don't want to stay with her on this earth father. Either she dies, or I do it to myself."*

*"Please come and see me this week in the rectory. We can work together to help you find a way out of this mess, without anyone having to die because of it."*

I never received a visit and it tears at my conscience to this day that I couldn't be of more help to this poor soul in anguish.

There have been many more souls I was not able to help, but there have also been ones I was able to guide back to moral health. This must be the way a doctor feels when he or she can't help someone about to face a life-threatening illness. There are medical miracles, I know, but I can only pray that in His wisdom, God helps those in moral danger who pray for His help in their times of spiritual need.

It was time for me to get ready for a good night's sleep. There was a message waiting for me, however, that was about to prevent that. Dr. Justin Daniels asked me to meet him at his office tomorrow morning after my regular confession schedule and Mass. Now what?

# Chapter 22

I did have a restless night, but no dreams that needed help in interpreting from my friend, Nicki.

There was no one waiting near the confessional, but as soon as I was seated, the door opened and a soft voice began:

*"Bless me, Father, for I have sinned. My last confession was two years ago. I have need of forgiveness for the following offenses:*

*I am currently employed by an accountant attorney who has asked me to look into his father's business. His father is a doctor in the city. The problem is…I feel torn between my loyalty to my employer and this doctor, his father, who has helped me in the past, with an unwanted pregnancy."*

*"How did this doctor help you?"* I asked gently, expecting the answer to be he performed an abortion.

*"Unfortunately, I lost the baby, and he was able to help me keep this a secret from the father."*

*"Did the doctor know who the father was?"*

*"Yes. It was his son, who was going through a divorce."*

*"Your sin is that you and his son committed adultery?"* I was trying to help this young woman face the truth.

*"My sin is that I found out that the doctor is giving out pain pills to his patients. I don't want to tell his son as this wasn't what the son wanted me to find out about his father."*

*"I hope you can tell me what the son wanted you to investigate about the father."*

*"He wanted me to find out who his father's brother is?"*

*"His brother?"*

"*Apparently, my employer had a visit from some detective who was investigating an old murder case, and he wanted to know about my employer's grandfather.*"

I was beginning to see a connection.

"*The detective let on that there was a child born to the doctor's sister many years ago, who was given up for adoption. My employer never knew about this.*"

"*Why is this so important to your employer, now?*" Did this young woman know that I was the child given up for adoption and that I was related her employer by blood?"

"*The attorney I work for wants to run for public office. He wants to make sure there are no unpleasant skeletons in his closet. He doesn't know his father hands out pain pills. I only found out because I went to the doctor's office, recently and talked with some of his patients in the waiting room. They're all elderly and think the doctor's a saint for giving them pills they don't have to have prescriptions for that take care of all their ailments. The doctor gives them the pain pills so they don't have to buy them off the street. They pay the doctor cash, with no questions asked. I told them I was the doctor's grand-daughter so they had no problem talking to me about every one of their grand-children and their ailments that needed pill power.*"

"*How did you know to come to me for confession?*"

I could see right through the girl's poor attempts to hide her employer's identity by citing his job as being an attorney. I knew she was referring to Jackson Daniels, a comptroller and an attorney.

"*I saw you, a few weeks ago having lunch in Niagara Falls, with a detective. This detective had been in to talk with my employer. You were obviously a priest, and I called the detective to ask him who you were and where you were assigned.*"

Her story was obviously so full of pot holes, I decided against cross-examining her.

*"You want to ask for absolution for...?"*

*"Hiding from my employer what I found out about his doctor-father dealing with pain pills. Hiding this information could hurt my employer in his bid for public office."*

I was mentally trying to picture this young woman. She must have been Jackson's secretary. The only thing familiar about her was her perfume. I believe it was the unique scent of *Chanel#5*.

*"Did you find out whether the doctor had a brother?"* I had to cut to the chase. I knew the young woman was getting nervous.

*"When I was called in to see the doctor, I panicked and said I was late for another appointment and would call again to set up a new appointment to see the Doctor next week."*

*"Did your employer ask you about what you had found out?"*

*"I lied and said the doctor told me he only had a son left on this earth. My employer became angry and said his father was hiding the fact that his brother was still alive."*

*"Did your employer tell you why he wanted to meet this brother?"*

*"All he said was that his father had never made any money having a small-time practice. If there was a relative still alive who could help fund his campaign efforts, he would like to know about him."*

*"Do you think you should tell your employer about his father and the pain pills?"*

*"I think I should, now. Maybe that would convince my employer not to run for office. The scandal would hurt his chances, for sure. It might even make him stop trying to find his father's supposed brother."*

*"Do you think this brother exists?"*

*"I don't know,"* The young woman was becoming agitated. *"Jack... my employer thinks he does."*

Her slip-up confirmed that her employer was, in fact, Jackson Daniels. I was relieved that Jackson thought the supposed living relative was a brother, and not a nephew...me.

*"Follow your conscience, in regard to your employer, before he stands naked before the public. Every second of his life will be examined, if he decides to run in the political arena. It takes courage to be a public figure, in today's world. It also may take a good deal of moral stamina to bury long ago dead bodies."*

*"I know what you mean, Father. I don't know anyone whose life is perfect. I believe I have to tell the truth to my employer and trust he'll know what to do with this information."*

When the young woman left the confessional, I stayed behind a while, with the lingering scent of *Chanel# 5*, to give her a chance to leave the church without me seeing her. I try to be discreet and look down when I leave the confessional, but sometimes, I do inadvertently, make eye contact with someone who has just confessed. Many of these guilty souls look like deer caught in the headlights of a car. If only they knew that most of the sins I hear are very common failings in judgment and results of poor choices. No one is perfect. Not anyone. And now I had to meet up with Justin Daniels, an imperfect doctor, who I'm sure has a perfect explanation for why his patients are getting pain pills so freely from his office.

The penance I had given the *Chanel #5* woman was to follow her conscience and do the hard thing in order to give her employer the opportunity to do the right thing, before it was all too late.

At least, the rest of my busy day would keep me from thinking about Jackson's secretary's confession and the big party I have to attend as the guest of honor. It was only two days away. I hoped I would come down with laryngitis or something before then.

## Chapter 23

"My son paid me a visit last evening, Rob. He said he knew you had been here earlier."

All of Dr. Daniels' patients were gone. His nurse was in his living quarters upstairs, warming up his dinner.

"I hope you can join me for a bite to eat, Rob. I eat quite early these days. My bed-time is getting earlier and earlier, too. I can barely make the 7:00 o'clock evening news. Not that I need to hear about all the nonsense wreaking havoc in today's world."

I wondered if he knew about the havoc his son was about to wreak.

"Lexie, my nurse," he explained, "is not only my receptionist, she's also a great chef. I pay her another salary, just so I can continue to have a hot meal almost every night. She loves my kitchen Tells me when she was growing up, her family was so poor, all they could afford were canned goods re-heated in a big tin pot that often was used again to make pop-corn for the evening snack."

I knew exactly the situation Justin was describing. I ministered to many people who had a hard time for a variety of reasons: lack of education; lack of role models; broken families, not to mention, drugs and alcohol.

"I have dinner plans, Justin," I regretfully admitted. I was beginning to enjoy the company of "my uncle;" someone older than myself, and probably a good deal wiser. "But, just out of curiosity, what will you be having?" I had to ask. "The aroma wafting downstairs smells enticingly like pot roast. Looks, sounds, and smells like Lexie made a great big leap from being poor to having a successful career and having a great talent as a cook."

"Thanks to you," Justin smiled slyly. "Apparently, she's friends with a young man you helped a great deal with the money from your trust fund. Does the name *Leo Jackson* ring a bell?"

"Ah. The Mission trust-fund I set up to help anyone who needed a financial ladder to climb up out of poverty through education."

"Exactly. I admire your philanthropic bent, Rob. I, also, have a way of helping those unable to help themselves."

"Lexie was able to go to nursing school because of your generosity. It's a shame they don't teach how to choose a life partner in school. She's going to make a big mistake marrying my son. I can't tell her not to, of course."

"Why not."

"I'm not at all sure she'd take my advice. She's love-sick. As a result, she can't see what sane people see."

I began laughing at his description of being "mad" about someone, or "madly" in love.

Justin also gave me the heads up about the pills he was giving his patients.

"My son found out from someone that I was giving pain-pills without prescriptions to many of my elderly patients who needed them to stay out of nursing homes and rehab centers. There was no way I was going to allow them to be at the mercy of street sellers. I didn't tell him I have a supplier who brings them across the river from Canada by means I don't care to divulge, even to you. I still charge $20.00 a visit, pills included. My son was incensed when I admitted to him that his accusation was correct. He wasn't upset by my giving out the pills, however. No. He was furious that I was charging so little. He actually told me I was robbing him of his inheritance by practically giving out pills that can cost more than $150 apiece, on the street."

I knew he was going to explain the pills now. It shocked me to know Jackson only wanted his father to sell the pills for more money, not stop giving them to his patients! I'm sure there are many people who look the other way when profit is involved. Money motivates so many devious actions.

"You're right, Justin. I didn't realize the pain-pill debacle has become so wide-spread because of addiction and the profit motive. It's devastating."

"Doesn't it gall you that the general public thinks poor people are the drug-pushers and takers? My own son, who works in City Hall, wants me to charge more so he can profit!"'"

"It galls me when all the ills and evils of society are blamed on those who have the least. It's easy to lay the blame for drug abuse on them. White collars never seem to get soiled for their part in the drug-trade."

"If only my son knew the kinds of pills I've been handing out, he'd be shown for what he is…a fool."

He ignored my asking what he meant by "the kind of pills," and continued his lecture on how the poor have been treated through the ages:

"When England first became industrialized, and Irish and Jewish immigrants were pouring into the already over-crowded urban centers, the slums were created, and the rich actually coined the word *slumming,* to describe their leisurely activity of visiting the slums to have a look at how the poor lived. The upper crust didn't want to believe that poverty was a vicious cycle caused by low wages and instead, blamed it on laziness and ignorance."

"Sounds like things haven't changed much as far as society's attitude toward the poor and even the refugees fleeing devastation."

"That's why I'm so very disappointed in my son, Jackson. He could make a difference with his political clout. But, I'm afraid he's in it for what he can gain for himself."

"Is that why you asked me to come by? To see if I could talk to your son about changing his priorities?"

"I wish it wasn't too late for that, Rob. No. I asked you to come by to warn you."

Justin suddenly looked as old as a ninety year -old could. He was weary and defeated.

"I wanted to warn you that Jackson found out that you're related to our family by blood. Somehow, his investigating came across your birth certificate that shows in black and white what I tried to keep from him all his life."

"That's probably why his secretary saw me having lunch in Niagara Falls. But, she wanted to…" I almost spilled out her confession to me about the pill problem, but stopped myself just in time. I wondered how she got hold of my birth certificate though. Did she ask the detective? My thoughts were interrupted by more of Justin's ranting:

"That poor girl. My immoral son got her pregnant a while back. She's in love with him, although I don't know how she can stand him. I'm sure there are other girls attracted to his good looks and heartless soul. They all must think they're the special ones who can get him to feel something. He can con a prostitute into paying him."

"You don't think much of your son, I'm afraid to note. But, does it bother your sense of morality that you're doing something illegal by passing out pain pills without prescriptions?"

I asked this gently. No accusatory tone, at all.

"I treat my patients as they need, Rob. They're not going out on the streets re-selling these pills for profit. They need them for their pains. Why should they be made to suffer because the bad people found another way to make money off the innocent?"

"But you could be jailed! Your patients could be jailed. Isn't this all dangerous?"

"We're already in jail, Rob. Thanks to old age, our bodies are our prisons. We all joke how prison could be our nursing homes, if we ever had to face legal issues. That really wouldn't be so bad, considering all the rights and privileges prisoners have today."

"When you explain it that way…I can see how your final judgement day may not be so bad either."

He laughed at my conclusion.

"Sure you can't have dinner with me, Rob?"

"I'll have to take a rain check. It seems like we could end up having quite a few animated discussions on morality, ethics, and practicality."

"Looking forward to it. Stimulating the mind keeps the bodily aches and pains at bay, and that's the main goal till the grim reaper takes his final swipe."

"Your sense of humor is morbid yet strangely refreshing, Justin."

"Glad you appreciate it. But truly heed my warning. Jackson is desperate for funds to feed his political ambitions. He's going to try and weasel his way into your trust fund."

"Thanks for the warning, but I can't even break into it without Board approval."

"Desperate times call for desperate measures, as the saying goes," Justin counseled. "He found a way to get a copy of your original birth certificate."

I couldn't help but accept that's why he felt no guilt about dispensing pills illegally to his patients.

"I have to ask if your nurse, cooking up that delicious dinner upstairs, knows about you dispensing pain pills."

"We've never formally discussed it. It would be unethical for me to involve her. She happens to be Jackson's secretary's sister. I suspect Lexie's the one who told Mandy about my secret enterprise. That's the most likely explanation as to how Jackson found out about the pills I dispense. I've never asked her. I had to pretend I didn't know Mandy when Lexie introduced me to her. Her pregnancy with Jackson's baby made us both pretend we had never met. But of course, I knew Mandy more intimately than even her own sister knows her."

"How could Lexie not know about this situation? I mean she is your nurse."

"I arranged to meet Mandy at the hospital clinic. 'Lexie must never learn that Jackson's the father of my baby,' she had pleaded."

"Why all the secrecy?"

"Rob, Lexie's engaged to Jackson. Mandy and he had an affair during his first marriage. Don't ask me how or why Jackson became involved with Lexie. It's too complicated for my old brain. All I know is Mandy doesn't want her sister to know about her affair with my son."

"I'd hate to be in the room when Lexie finds out about Mandy and her fiancé. Those things are always eventually revealed, as I can confirm by meeting you."

"Now you know why all the secrecy," he laughed. "That's another reason why my son is so despicable to me. I've been in hospitals where a mother has just given birth and the father's girlfriends come in and try to tear the new mother's hair out. My son is one of those men who sleeps around, leaving broken women everywhere he's been; not having any decency about who is being hurt. And the women…well…they must be poor souls lacking any self-esteem or don't have any sense that they're being used."

"Like Lexie and Mandy." I commented. "I think because they grew up in such a poor environment, they were able to help themselves out of the poverty cycle, successfully, but the damage done to their self-esteem and self-respect was never fully repaired."

"That may be true, Rob. However, women from every walk of life have been conned into thinking they've found true love with unscrupulous men. It's a shame I bear, knowing that my son is one of those cads. An old-fashioned derogatory term that never goes out of style, I'm afraid."

I knew that he was right. And I knew men take advantage of those weaknesses in women who are simply wanting to love and be loved. Men like Jackson, whose own father can't stand to be around him. Men can see the superficiality in other men. I wish women could too.

Women come to confession, generally, to complain that they can no longer love or live with a husband who is cheating, is always drunk, beats them, or is neglectful in so many husbandly ways.

I try to console them and offer them names of marriage counselors. I really want to tell them to throw the bums out. But this isn't Catholic or Christian. I tell them they can come to me in confession, or even the rectory. I try to medicate their souls. They're living nightmare lives. I pray for them. I even pray that the Church eases the divorce laws. I won't live long enough to see that happen, so I listen and offer annulment advice.

When the men come to confession, they usually confess actual sins of theft, revenge, hatred, blasphemy, and lying. Almost never do they confess to adultery. I know they commit this sin, but they might refer to it as cheating. It sounds less evil. They don't want to admit that most wives are on to it. They refuse to see the damage it does to the marriage. They hate admitting it is corrupting their own souls.

They call it cheating. They're shocked when divorce papers are served.

But I'm still in shock in discovering my entire life is one based on re-payment of a debt my father owed to Justin's father. I was a plain simple parish priest. Within the last few hours, I've learned I was adopted, have ties to the mob, have a living uncle, and a cousin who might become a villain in my remaining life story. I've also become acquainted with a new cast of characters whose names I'll have to keep straight, thanks to my new relations: Justin Daniels, Martin Foster, Lexie, Mandy, and God knows how many more will be cast in my new role as Jackson's cousin?

## Chapter 24

I kept wondering, later that evening, how Leo, and others my trust fund had helped, were able to keep from slipping back into the old ways of their neighborhoods that often dragged back those who tried to better themselves.

There are over sixty gangs in Buffalo! They're located in close vicinity to the Mission. It's a miracle it isn't robbed every hour. But, many of the gangs have family members that are helped by this island of care. They leave it alone.

Jackson Daniels, obviously thought he had hit pay dirt in checking out its parameters for drug activity. Lenore would never stand for that. She helps those willing to help themselves. Those who have no desire for honest work because of the lure of easy cash, turn to the gangs...not the Mission. Old friends and loyalties were often the bait that drew back those who felt they didn't deserve better lives or who found a normal work schedule too much.

For whatever reason, there are successful, even wealthy people, who made it out of the welfare cycle, but can't seem to stay away from those that are still stuck. By coincidence, before I settled into a pre-dinner nap, my voice mail informed me that Leo Jackson had called and would like a return call.

I was looking forward to asking him that very question, nagging at me for so very long. How was he able to climb out of poverty and stay away, while others seemed stuck there, or sucked back in, no matter how much help they received.

Leo was not in when I tried to return his call.

A woman answered, and asked if she could take a message.

I told her I was returning Leo's call, and wanted to know if she knew the nature of it.

Good humor was seeping into my personal space, once again. So much has happened this last week, I was getting all riled up. I just needed to get through the Saturday shindig and all my problems would be over. I could relax all day Sunday, and even thought about driving to Niagara-on-the Lake for a preview of the Shaw Festival plays I so looked forward to each year.

Nicki and her husband had treated me to Shaw's *St. Joan*, a few years back. It's going to be repeated on this year's schedule. The play is wonderful. It's refreshing to listen to intelligent dialogue whose meaning stays with you after the performance.

The town is charming as well and very British. Tea and crumpets, flowers, everywhere filled the streets. People from all over the world come to see one or more of the dramas presented each year at the numerous theatres scattered throughout the tiny village on Lake Ontario.

The drive along the Niagara Gorge is magnificent in its own right. Deep blue-green water bordered by green trees, walking trails, picnic tables, make the trip worth the short drive over the Border.

My thoughts were interrupted by the feminine voice on the other line. She probably thought I had hung up on her. Lately, I drift off into another world, as I had just done.

I was disoriented, and almost hung the phone up.

"Hello? Hello? Is this Father Sullivan?" the woman's voice asked.

"So sorry. I have an older phone. It must have disconnected us for a bit. I'm here now."

Thank God, we weren't speaking to each other in person. I would have been supremely embarrassed. I have to be careful about drifting off. It doesn't happen much, unless I'm on the phone.

There I go again. I pulled my attention back to the receiver. "Yes…Miss… Do I know to whom I'm speaking?"

"Not really. I'm Leo Jackson's fiancé. I know he called to set up an appointment with you so we could talk about our wedding plans. We'd like to be married at the Mission church and would like to discuss all the pre-nuptial details to make this happen,"

And your name is?" I grabbed a pen and pad of paper, to make sure I could take some notes. It helped to focus on something definite when speaking to a faceless voice. I'm surprised I don't dose off in the confessional, when I can't see the person confessing. At least, I hope I didn't.

I'm Melissa James. I grew up with Leo, Mandy, and Lexie. We're from the old neighborhood, stayed friends, and now Leo and I are going to tie the knot.

"Well, Melissa James. I'm looking forward to meeting you. Do you work with Leo?"

"Yep. I mean, Yes, Father. He got me a job as an apprentice pattern cutter and we've been cutting our own pattern ever since."

Melissa sounded like a delightful young woman. It was wonderful that Leo was planning on getting married. So many young people today consider this custom to be old-fashioned and impractical. I still adhered to the principle that if children were going to be brought into this world, both parents were necessary ingredients for successful batches of offspring. Baking delicate souffles that rise perfectly is difficult, takes patience, and the correct proportions of ingredients. Even then, many still fail. Burning batches of cookies is caused by neglect and indifference. It's nearly impossible for me not to allude to metaphors that weren't related to food. This has always been my go-to way of describing my beliefs during sermons and counseling session.

"I always feel hungry, after Mass, and your homily," many of my parishioners have joked.

"My pleasure, as well as yours," I would counter.

But getting back to Melissa… before she hung up on my mind's meandering, once again…"If you're free this week or next, you and Leo can drop by the rectory any time before lunch, and after Mass. I should be here, no problem."

"Thanks, Father. Leo and I will be sure to come by. If you see Mandy or Lexie, tell them I said *Hi.*"

"Aren't you coming to the big bash with Leo this Saturday? I assume you're going to be his date. I believe Lexie will be there with her fiancé, Jackson Daniels. And perhaps, even Lexie's sister, Mandy, will also be making an appearance."

"That's right. Mandy is Jackson's secretary. Small world, isn't it, Father?" I detected a bit of hesitation and even sarcasm in her voice.

"At least Buffalo is," I replied. "Never know who you're going to meet wherever, whenever."

"So right, Father. But I've got to run now. I want to finish laying out this pattern before, Leo, the boss, gets on my case. We love each other outside of work, but at work, he's like his namesake...a real Lion."

"Looking forward to meeting you, Melissa. Now get back to work."

I was going to ask Nicki on Saturday, if she would like to accompany me for lunch at one of the fine restaurants, either along the way to her vineyard, or in town. She would know the best spots for sure. I would ask her if she too, found her mind drifting from the present. She's only two years younger than me. My phone conversation with Leo's fiancé made me aware of how disconcerting it must be for others when my mind decides to go off on tangents, unrelated to the current conversation.

Physically, I still feel pretty good. I take long walks and indulge my wandering mind. But, lately, I find that my memories were taking up much more of my time than was needed to focus on the problems I still need to solve for the souls I'm committed to shepherd. At least I'm still able to keep straight the names of my old friends and new acquaintances. And, it seems nothing really shocks me anymore. I've heard most everything humans are capable of in the confessional. Things are still good.

I was feeling better and better each minute. A quick short nap would complete my well-being. It was great how young love can make a dreary day full of sunshine. I think Lenore mentioned that Leo would be bringing his girl to the Anniversary party. She did sound quite nice over the phone. Could be another success story of someone able to leave the dregs of poverty to begin a better life. Leo and Melissa will definitely be able to be racked up on the side of success stories. I don't even want to think of those that just couldn't make it. As far as I know, only one or two were drawn back to the seedy side of life.

I hoped Marcus and Antoine, the would-be gangsters, who tried to rob Norm's Pizzeria, could keep walking the straight line. I want to rack their successes alongside Leo and Melissa's. Time would tell. I should be able to last another five years at least, to see more fruits of my trust fund blossom and take root. Look at my Uncle Justin, I chuckled, out loud to myself. Ninety, and still going strong, taking care of patients as old and older than me.

# Chapter 25

My nap quieted my thoughts, but not before I thought of the irony of how things that astounded or shocked me when I was younger, no longer have the same impact on my peace of mind. If I had found out about my birth parents being different from those who raised me, I might have spent years tracking down the truth, wasting valuable time. My life was not wasted pursuing the past. For this, I am grateful to my father and mother for keeping the truth from me. It's also ironic that Justin's son, Jackson, knows my secret past, and might use it to steal from the trust fund I was so meticulous in setting up, thanks to the advice of Lenore and her husband. He may try to lay claim to it, after I pass on, but I have no intention of doing so for at least five more years. By that time, he would have spent more money in legal fees trying to break that trust fund instead of cashing in on it.

I fell asleep with a clear mind, conscience, and positive outlook for the rest of my life. God-willing, of course.

Lenore's call ended my nap. She was setting up her agenda.

"I hope you're well-rested. I'll be over tomorrow or Friday with plans for re-modeling your decrepit rectory."

"As a matter of fact, I'm feeling fit as a fiddle, Lenore, and am looking forward to seeing what fresh new ideas you have for this crypt."

"Dare I ask why? Did Tina drop off an apple pie for you to devour all by yourself?"

"Did she say she was going to?" I asked, hopefully.

"No, silly. I was being funny."

"Never, ever joke about food, Lenore. It might put me in an awful mood. But, I do have some welcome news. Leo's fiancé called to set up a meeting to discuss their up-coming nuptials."

"Really? I'm surprised. Leo never said a word about this to me, and I just spoke with him yesterday, to confirm his attendance at the Anniversary Party on Saturday."

"There you go again…trying to stifle my mood."

"Rob, stop it! You didn't have to lift a finger for all this. We girls have been planning and doing everything ourselves. All you have to do is show up. Is that so much to ask?"

"The difference is you all enjoy this type of busy work. I hate all that pomp and circumstance. That's why my Mass celebrations are a half hour or less. I keep my sermons short, sweet, and to the point. The highpoint is the Eucharist…not me, up at the altar, acting all holy."

"If the Pope could hear you now. You'd be de-frocked for sure."

We both laughed, knowing our banter was just that. Not a single argument ever dented our relationship. Come to think of it, none of my girls and I were ever on the outs. We did have lively discussions, but never insulted or dis-respected each other's points of view. Maybe we should go into marriage counseling, or better yet, politics.

"When did you say Leo and his fiancé were meeting with you?"

"I didn't. I told Melissa she could drop by with Leo any time before Saturday. I forgot to write down any specific day or time. I'll be here, hiding out before the big day. And I am sorry, Lenore, for trying to dampen your parry-planning spirits. I do appreciate all you girls trying to make my 50th year as a priest, special."

"Well, it is…special. I want to thank you for all you've done for me and Jaime, and I know the others are also grateful for your help, guidance, and spiritual care."

"Okay. That's enough for now. Save it for the toasts." It would have been better if all this flattery heaped upon me was a large mound of buttery mashed potatoes, instead. Thinking of food, I asked Lenore why she wasn't meeting Shelly, Tina, and me for dinner tonight.

"I have too many last-minute details to attend to. I can never relax and eat when I have a list of things I have to do, swarming through my mind."

"That's how you keep your girlish, figure. Keeping busy keeps you svelte."

"That's the nicest thing you've said to me in a long time, Rob. I will take the compliment and bid you adieu."

Lenore had a valid point. My girls always did so much for me, I've neglected to tell them how much I appreciate them. And here they are planning this elaborate shin-dig to honor me! I'll make a point of praising them tonight. Never would I want to take them for granted.

My girls are all like little sisters to me. I have male friends I do manly things with, like going to see the Bills, Sabres, and even a few baseball games in the summer. But, sitting around at dinner, talking about feelings and why people behave the way they do is not really the masculine modus operandi. Plus, I don't have any man friends who cook or bake for me.

I've seen retired men sitting around fast-food joints, discussing sports and politics. I know they don't discuss wives or family problems. Women can't seem to get enough of analyzing relationships. It's ironic how we can't live without each other, but complain about it in so many ways.

It was time for me to get ready for our dinner. We were going to Falletta's, in Clarence, where the cooking is home-made, almost as good as Tina's. She and Shelly had called Uber to drive the ten miles to the restaurant. I love Buffalo's set-up, in that one is able to get from one end of the city to the other, and even to its suburbs in a half hour or less. This is probably why, as Melissa and I had agreed in our phone conversation, that it's easy to know the same people. In Buffalo, there are fewer than six degrees of separation.

I looked around the rectory office before leaving to await the Uber. It certainly did need refurbishing. There were cracks in its poor plaster, reminding me of my own facial cracks. I'm not really a vain person, but sometimes the mirror shocks me into reality. I am growing older. I've been blessed with good health, so my outward appearance isn't that important to me. Sucking in my expanding gut, I was looking forward to filling it with delicious pasta.

## Chapter 26

"Lenore told me you were in a good mood, Rob. It seems like it hasn't faded," Shelly smiled.

"It's always happy time, for you, at dinner," Tina offered, also smiling.

"I'm afraid I've behaved like a complete spoiled brat, girls," I admitted, sheepishly. "You and Lenore have worked ceaselessly to make sure the party being given in my honor at the Central Terminal is a smashing success. I have been anything but honorable. I humbly apologize."

"Wow!" Tina marveled. "What brought this change of heart on? If I didn't know better, I'd have assumed you found a new love to brighten your spirits."

"Actually…it is love," I grinned, enjoying the confused look on both women's lovely faces. I decided I wouldn't be coy. I'd put them through enough.

"Leo Jackson and his fiancé, Melissa, are going to meet with me to discuss their up-coming nuptials. Both of them are success stories, having made good use of the money from my trust fund to climb up the ladder of success."

"See, Rob?" Shelly chirped. "You and your money have helped so many it would be selfish of you not to allow them to thank you at this mile-stone of your life. People don't always want to just take. They also like to thank and try to give back in some way; paying their success forward."

"I still believe in the goodness of most people, Shelly. It will be good for everyone to meet with each other on Saturday to see they're not the only ones who need helping hands. I hope Antoine and Marcus, with their mothers, will be there?"

"Oh yes," Tina said. "And they've gotten together to make sure there will be enough of their famous barbecue ribs to over-shadow the hot dogs and wings you've requested."

"Perfect," I glowed. "This amazing pasta tastes even better now with that good news."

"So far, three hundred people are expected to drop in. We have planned for a total of five hundred. Stragglers are always welcome. Anyone else you'd like us to contact?" Shelly was in charge of RSVP'S. I almost responded that the number expected was already too many but I wisely held my tongue.

"And don't worry. All you have to do is shake hands and smile."

"Oh, I'll be making the rounds," I said. "As long as I can also make the food rounds."

"Of course." Tina explained. She was in charge of ordering all the food. "We'll have food stations set up. No one will have to sit at formal tables."

"That makes me feel way better," I admitted.

"I've already printed out the pamphlets about the need to preserve the grand old train station. I've kept my promise about making this a kind of fund-raising awareness for the Central Terminal. I'm hoping someone you know with deep pockets will be attending and have his or her interest perked up in seeing financial profit in a total re-hab of the building." Shelly knew the entire history of all the important Buffalo structures.

"Why is the terminal so historically important, Shelly?" I asked.

"I'll tell you while we eat our cannoli." And she did, and it was very interesting: "Thank God, we aren't expecting the 2,200 guests the Chamber of Commerce feted at the grand opening luncheon in 1929. We've agreed that this is going to be an awareness event and a wake-up call to all Western New Yorkers. We can save this building, if we all put our heads, hearts, and pocket-books together. How else are we going to get the elite of Buffalo down to this part of the city, if not to honor one of their own? I hate to have to remind you, dear friend, but you are part of Buffalo's upper class. You come from money, even though you've made it possible to give most of it away. Your mother has her picture up at the 21st Century Club, for heaven's sake, for her ceaseless dedication."

One doesn't interrupt Shelly when she's on a roll:

"That 15 story office tower that once employed 1500 people could be re-converted into offices or apartments. The concourse, where we'll be holding your anniversary/benefit is the greatest public space in Buffalo."

"I know I've met a lot of people, Shelly, but holding this party in the largest public space in Buffalo? Isn't this a bit pretentious?"

I was almost tempted to tell her that that picture is not of my real mother. But what purpose would it serve? I didn't interrupt Shelly's flow of selling points for the Central Terminal's preservation.

"Lenore is in love with the Roman arched windows, balconies, and Guastavino tile lining the Terminal's ceiling and walls; Not to mention all the beautiful marble. She said modern-day mansions lack these exquisite features created just before the Depression of the 1930's. Loss of disposable income made travel a luxury and made it impossible to sustain a profit. WWII soldiers were its main benefactors, coming to and from their battle stations. At least they had a beautiful place to return home to. I'm no Jackie Kennedy, but she helped save Grand Central in NYC when she said that if we don't preserve the past, we can't have much hope for our future."

Shelly's eyes would burn with passion when she talked about preserving our city's historic buildings. I liked to compare her with St. Joan who fought for her city. Thankfully, we don't burn people at the stake for their beliefs, anymore.

"I know how much you love the past, Shelly" I said. "I think the biggest hurdle to preserving that beautiful Art Deco masterpiece is its location. It's not far from the Mission and the surrounding neighborhood is like a third world country."

"That's another selling point, Rob," she protested. "Look what happened when Larkin Square began to re-do its environment with grass, and food trucks, and places for people to sit, eat, and listen to music and lectures? The entire neighborhood is starting to be re-born. We have to end having beautiful streets surrounded by pockets of urban decay."

"Shelly's right," Tina added. "One small stone causes infinite ripples. And think what a ripple effect that huge stone would create?"

"You've convinced me, ladies. I see your excellent points. We should put our heads together and really make a list of people who could help make it happen financially, and creatively."

"See?" Shelly was beaming. "It takes women to make the world go 'round. We only need to push our men around more to get some traction."

"I'm serious, Shelly. I've been thinking of some way to help keep people stay on the right path, once they've started on the difficult journey to success without guideposts. The terminal could be a central place to train, employ, and even provide housing for the hundreds of people we haven't been able to reach with my generous but limited trust fund and the short but effective reach of the Mission."

"Guess, the trains will start running again, huh, Rob?"

"Yep, and this time, I didn't even need to use a food metaphor to make my point."

Both women seemed puzzled by my statement.

"No matter. It's an inside joke. The Holy Spirit has indeed been a dinner guest tonight. I'll gladly pay the tab."

"You always do, Rob," Tina said. "But, I promise you, next week, after all the hullabaloo, I'll cook you up your favorite dish."

"Which is?"

"Really? You know whatever is put in front of you, as long as it's home-cooked, is your favorite."

"So true," I laughed. "Seriously, though, what do you think is my favorite dish of all my favorites?"

"If I had to choose from your vast list, I would probably say spaghetti, pizza, Asian cuisine, anything from the pork, chicken, beef family, as well as from the spud plant, anything with gluten, and for dessert, apple pie, for sure."

Shelly clapped her hands with approval. "Well done, Tina."

"I beg to differ," I quipped. "I do not like my beef well-done."

Of course, they groaned in unison. But they loved me, corniness and all.


That evening, I said my evening prayers, grateful for the women in my life who have enriched it in so many ways. It made me realize why Jesus enjoyed having women around him, wherever he traveled, spreading his message of love and peace. I don't believe he ever considered them lesser than men. He spoke with them as equals. They were the last people with him at the crucifixion, lovingly tending to his broken body. His apostles were all in hiding. They were holed up in some attic, fearing arrest by the authorities because of their friendship with Jesus.

The women were the first persons the resurrected Christ appeared to:

Mary Magdalene, Mary, his own mother and the mother of James, Salome, and Joanna.

Men forget that it's through women they are born. A seed can be planted, but it may not bear fruit. This, I knew, would be the topic of my Sunday sermon.

I wrote my musings down in the notebook I kept by my bedside. Nicki had urged me to do so in connection with my dreams. She said memories of night dreams, quickly fade upon waking. My notebook was becoming filled with strange dreams, but also with kernels of inspiration that made my sermons somewhat relevant and interesting, at least to me. I usually took this written record to my study in the rectory to compose my thoughts and my sermons on Friday mornings. I would have to begin the process tomorrow, instead. Friday would be filled with Lenore's re-decorating schemes, and hopefully, Melissa and Leo's visit to discuss their marriage plans.

Saturday afternoon was inching closer by the minute. I could get through it. My girls won't abandon me. And I won't disappoint them.

And with that, we said good-night, promising to meet at the Central Terminal an hour before the guests were asked to begin to arrive at 2:00 PM.

"Don't worry, Rob," Shelly said. "You'll be tucked into bed by 10:00 PM."

"Eight hours of partying!" I complained.

"That's including the post-party review at my house, with any left-overs you may feel the need to consume."

"Alright, then. I won't complain anymore."

They knew appealing to my appetite was the way to break through any resistance I might put up.

# Chapter 27

My Thursday was free after Mass, so I decided to pay my new friend, Dr. Daniels a visit. I knew he was seeing patients till late afternoon, so I timed my visit to arrive at around 3:30. It would almost be time for high tea. Hopefully, his nurse/chef, Lexie, would be able to whip us up some nice little sandwiches. I'll stop by Mazurek's bakery on South Park to pick up some pastries, that aren't too dainty.

I was able to miss the afternoon rush hour and found a great parking space almost in front of the Delaware mansion that was Dr, Daniels' office and home. I believe his son, Jackson, was raised in that home, and it also may have been the office of Jason L. Daniels, my father's business associate. I know the original homestead was in Lewiston, as Detective Sander s had informed me.

Entering the waiting room, I was very surprised to see the detective, sitting in one of the leather chairs, casually leafing through a magazine. He looked up, and was pleased to see me, though not surprised.

"Are you investigating Dr. Daniels now?"

"No," he laughed. "I'm here for treatment. An old knee injury causes me severe pain at times."

"You take pain pills," I asked tentatively.

"No. Justin has this new procedure using radio waves to deaden the nerves that cause pain. It's just been approved by the FDA, though it's been used a few years as a test procedure."

"Do you know Justin because of your investigation into his father's past dealings with the mob from Lewiston and the murder of your half-sister?"

"That's right," he admitted. "We've become friends, and I believe you and he have too."

"I've just come to know him, thanks to your investigation. You know he's my uncle?"

"We've discussed this, and I'm very aware of your ties to him. The only one who doesn't know is his son, Jackson,"

"That's where I have some information for you. Jackson found out after investigating me on his own. He told his father so just the other day."

Martin denied giving a copy of my original birth certificate to anyone. So, I still didn't know how Jackson got it.

"What does he intend to do with this information?"

"Justin thinks he's going to try and break into my trust fund as one of the legitimate heirs to the fortune, to fund his political ambitions."

"So, you know that Jackson's own father detests him?"

"I do, but is there more to this story than Justin told me?"

"There is, but I'll leave that to him for the reveal. It's not my place."

"And with that, welcome my old and new friends." Justin had appeared in the doorway to his inner sanctum and over-heard the last statement.

"I was hoping for some company, today. Spring has made me feel chipper. While I tend to Martin's knee, why don't you run upstairs, Rob, and ask Lexie to prepare some of those roast beef sliders I've been saving. There's some freshly ground horseradish from the Broadway Market. We'll have some snacks and some chats."

This sounded a lot more appetizing to me than cucumber sandwiches.

"I'm on it. Point out the stairway to heaven."

# Chapter 28

Lexie heard my approach. She was in the kitchen, already plating up the small kimmelweck rolls, and warming up the gravy for the roast beef.

"Do you prefer cold or hot sandwiches, Father Rob; au jus, or with gravy?"

"One of each, please. They're kinda small and together, they'll make one larger sandwich."

" I was told about your appetite," she laughed.

"From whom, may I ask?"

"Leo is a friend of mine from the old neighborhood. We even went to school together. That is, when Leo went to school."

"He's really come a long way, don't you think?"

Lexie was a very attractive strawberry blond. She resembled her sister, Mandy, in height and complexion. But, Mandy's hair was cut in a fashionable sleek bob. that looked almost like a mahogany helmet. Both were slender, with enhanced attributes added to their behinds and fronts. The Kardashians still dominated the style sense or nonsense of young women. It was impossible for natural bodies to have such small waists and enormous breasts and butts. I never really judge appearances. I merely comment on them, mostly to myself.

"Leo is making quite a career for himself in the fashion world. Who would have thought it back in the day. Do you know he's started his own fashion line?" Lexie sounded impressed.

"I hadn't heard. He's coming to see me, probably tomorrow, so I can ask him all about it." I didn't want to gossip about his being engaged. Perhaps it wasn't official yet.

"My sister knows Leo, too. She works for Dr. Daniels' son, Jackson, in City Hall. Jackson and I are engaged. I want my sister to stand up for my wedding, but she's refused." She frowned and quickly added, "Now why am I telling you all this? It's really silly that I'm telling you these things. I hardly know you at all."

"It's my face," I said, trying to ease her embarrassment. "Even strangers come up to me in the super market and start telling me things from their personal inventory of life events."

"It certainly is your face," Justin said. He and Martin had come upstairs and heard my last comment.

"Just what is it about me, Justin, that makes people want to open up their private diaries to me?"

"You have an honest face and an approachable bearing. You look interested in what people are saying, and make laser-like eye contact with them, and they feel like prying themselves open to you. Am I right Lexie?"

"I think so, Dr. Daniels. Father Rob makes me feel comfortable. Like you do as a doctor. I feel like I can trust you guys."

"How about me, Miss Lexie?" Martin asked. "Do I inspire confidence.?"

"Hmmm, I think you seem to be looking for answers. not offering safe havens."

I could see why Justin enjoyed having Lexie around. She was young, beautiful, friendly, smart, and had a great sense of humor and honesty. I wondered about whether she was also a trusted confidante of the doctor's, concerning his distribution of pills, so freely. It would be a waste if she married Jackson, that was something I was certain of.

"I also believe, Detective, that you can read minds, so people don't feel comfortable under your gaze."

We all laughed. But it is true what she said about me. I've been told before, that people seem to feel easy in opening up to me, even when I'm not wearing my Roman collar. One time, in line at the super market, a woman behind me, asked if I had a son. Before I could answer, she said, "If you do, I feel sorry for you. Why anyone would want children is beyond me." I felt it better to remain silent but offered a sympathetic look. "He was a good kid till he got mixed up with this girl on Facebook. Now all he wants to do is sit in his room and text with her. I found out she doesn't even live in this State!"

It was my turn to check out, so all I could do is say, "That Internet is going to cause lots of problems."

I knew this would open up a whole new can of worms. I was right.

The check-out woman agreed. She and the poor woman behind me continued their diatribe as I made my way out of the store. I knew the end of her story was that the kid would set up a meeting with the girl from out of State. A date, place, and time, in secret, of course. Only God would know whether this would be a set-up or a legitimate date. Being a parent in the modern world is definitely not easy when there were so many avenues for kids to travel down and hide their adventures from adults.

"I've made the platter of roast beef sliders, Dr. Daniels. There are hot ones with gravy, or au jus, and cold ones. Father Rob brought these pastry hearts from the bakery for your sweet tooths."

"Thanks so much, Lexie. You are just what the doctor ordered."

"Another corny remark like that might make us lose our appetite," Martin joked.

"Never," I quipped. "Nice talking with you Lexie. Are you coming to my… ahem…party on Saturday with Jackson?"

"We plan to. I just hope Jackson doesn't leave me alone too much to meet and shake everyone's hand. There's going to be some important people there, I hear."

"Everyone's important, Lexie. But, I'll make sure to rescue you if I see you abandoned," I volunteered.

Lexie left for the day, leaving the three new amigos alone with some delicious beef-on-weck sliders. We were enjoying the savory taste, but I noticed a slight frown on Justin's forehead

"Everything okay, Justin?" I asked.

"My nurse, Lexie, is such a sweet girl. Way too good for the likes of Jackson."

I remained silent, not wanting to stir up the negativity Justin felt toward his only son.

"I know all about this situation, Rob," Martin admitted. "If you want to elaborate more on your feelings, Justin, so our friend, Father Rob can understand them more, it could free your pent-up emotions."

"I don't want to ruin anyone's enjoyment of these delicious sandwiches right now. But after we begin to digest, I'll explain my disgust. So, let's eat, relax, and I'll be in a better frame of mind to explain when my belly's full of goodness."

"I can understand those feelings," I said, with a mouthful, trying to lighten the mood. It worked. We spent the next half hour savoring the tender beef and laughing at our eye-watering results after biting into mounds of sharp horseradish.

Strong coffee was next, accompanying the buttery flakiness of glazed hearts from the bakery.

"Those radio waves on your knee help with your pain?" I asked Martin.

"Sure does. Lasts up to eight months for me. I'd be willing to pay the three grand it costs for each treatment, but Justin, here, charges me only $500."

I wondered if he knew about the pills Justin freely dispensed to his other pain-riddled patients. It wasn't my place to put either of them on the spot by asking. My only concern was where the poor souls who were patients would find another source for easing their pain, after Justin passed on. Would they have to turn to street sellers, then?

"I know what you're thinking, Rob." The good doctor seemed to be reading my mind. "You don't see things turning out well for my patients after I'm gone or arrested."

I looked at Martin. He was serenely munching his pastry. Apparently, he was aware of the pill situation.

"My patients are conscious of this possibility. They can't afford the radio waves right now to ease their pain, but hopefully, Medicare will pick up most of the cost now that it's FDA approved. The clamor would be deafening if they don't. Plus, it's a viable response to the opioid epidemic. Fewer pills on the market, mean less people becoming addicted to them."

"I was on the pills, myself, Rob, before I was willing to try the radio wave," Martin stated.

"So, Justin isn't doing anything illegal?"

"No. Neither is his source. As a physician, he is simply following his oath. There is no reason for me to question his source or his distribution policy."

"I have to admit that makes me feel much better about all this."

"Ethics and morality have nothing to do with easing pain, Rob." Justin said. "It's the greed that makes some use this as a way to exploit the pain of people. Making money off pain is immoral. That's one of the reasons I can't stand Jackson. He's trying to make me into a drug dealer who will charge enormous prices for pills, so he can profit from it."

"Is he that desperate for money?" I asked.

"It's not so much the money…it's what money can buy him: influence, power, prestige, respect, all the things he's craved but was never able to work for in an honest way."

"And he thinks getting elected to political office will be his genie in the bottle, granting his every wish?"

"Exactly. It's the perfect job for people who do little to influence much."

"Do you think he can pull it off; getting elected?"

"It costs tons of cash to run campaigns nowadays. He hasn't won the endorsement of an established political party, and even if he had, those big pockets won't open if he has no capital of his own to put up. Unfortunately, only rich people in this society are taken seriously. Mere good ideas aren't enough. People worship money more than they do honesty. If you are a wonderful person, that's nice. If you are a rich person, no matter that you're not too nice...you have value in the eyes of the public as someone who knows how to make the American dream come true."

"I never thought of the political scene like that, Justin, but what you say makes perfect sense."

I knew my father would have been delighted if I had entered politics, instead of the priesthood. Unfortunately, my past as a juvenile delinquent put the kibosh on that. Just another disappointment I offered as a son. Was I as bad as Justin's Jackson? I hoped not.

"Throw in a bit of anger at the establishment," Martin commented, "and you have the perfect politician who has made it in the private sector, and the gullible public thinks he can make it happen for you, as a poor slob, living pay check to pay check. They really believe that their lives will become better, at least economically, if the system is turned inside out by someone who knows how to use it."

"Then that's why Jackson needs money. He needs to prove he's worthy enough to represent the people? Ordinary people."

"Exactly. Ordinary people worship celebrities and money. That's why so many have turned away for making honest livings. They find ways to make street money more profitable and don't have to pay taxes in the bargain. This is the way to live the new American dream of becoming rich and famous."

"Justin, is this why your son has brought you so much disappointment? You don't believe he's behaving as an honest person. You think he's using politics to get ahead for his own personal gain?"

"Rob, I'm going to tell you a story. Martin already knows it, and maybe you do too. I've already told you about Mandy and her affair with Jackson. Lexie doesn't know it all yet. She's going to marry the sonofabitch. And, sad to say, he really is rotten"

Justin's living room was more like a study. The walls were lined with books, and the wing-back chairs were made of sinkable comfortable leather. The round coffee table held our plates and there was a carafe for coffee refills, which we all did, before Justin proceed to tell an amazing tale of sad intrigue.

# Chapter 29

"My first wife, Ellie was a gem. She and I met in high school when we were enrolled at Park School. We came from affluent parents who strongly believed in education being the way to improve society, as a whole. At least my mother did. They were community-minded and wanted us to become leaders in Buffalo, but also anywhere else we chose to live.

Ellie's father had made his money from his father's business ties with a company which did Great Lakes shipping during its heyday. As you know, my father also had ties with the mob family in Lewiston, and had become an attorney. My mother was associated with the ladies who belonged to the Twentieth Century Club. They held fundraisers, continuously, for worthy projects and helped bring culture to Buffalo's society by hosting distinguished speakers. Robert Frost lectured there, and Theodore Roosevelt was a guest with his daughter, Alice. My wife was very active, behind the scenes with the other club members in seeing that the responsibility of the wealthy to contribute to society was always carried out."

"Somehow that ideal philosophy has faded." I interjected.

"My belief is that with the tax system, set up the way it is, the wealthy feel their fair share is already being spread out throughout the country. Charity has died with the Federal, State, and County tax collections. Philanthropy is scarce in the upper echelons. But that is a great discussion to have at our next meeting, perhaps next Thursday?"

"Same place, same time, new refreshments?"

We all laughed at our decision to hold weekly talk sessions. This was going to be a very nice weekly interlude for all of us.

"I'm sorry, Justin. Please continue your story. My interruptions will cease and desist immediately."

"No matter, Rob, I was beginning to wander away from my main story, by a side-line into my mother and first wife's lives."

He got up and went to his bookcase, which held a liquor cabinet at its base. For a 90-year old, he was quite spry. I hoped I had inherited some of those genes.

"Are either of you in a hurry this afternoon?"

Neither Martin nor I complained about the time, as he began pouring each of us a snifter of honey brandy.

"Good for the digestion, and courage for me to continue."

So far, his story was nothing I had not been surprised about. Rich kids marrying rich kids. The next part was a stunner.

## Chapter 30

The story Justin proceeded to tell took about an hour. We all felt drained after it was revealed why he was unable to love his son, Jackson.

After his first wife passed away, from cancer, Justin felt hopelessly alone. She was diagnosed and was gone within six months. He told us she had had stomach pains, but considered it a type of indigestion; nothing to worry about. The shock was traumatic. He withdrew and almost over-dosed himself with anti-depressants. But, his son, Charley saved him from going under. He knew Ellie would never forgive him for making their son, totally parent-less.

I didn't know what it was to lose a loving spouse, but I did feel deep sorrow for those who have. My strongest prayers are for those coping with loss of loved ones.

Justin continued, "Ellie's friends came by almost daily to comfort me and even tried to entice me to form a new relationship, with one of the women who had recently been divorced."

The part of his story which shocked me was that Jackson was not an only child. Ellie and he had raised a son who was 13, when Ellie passed away.

I was able to keep my mouth shut until all of Justin's story was out in the open, but so many questions arose from this revelation.

"Alice Wicks was the woman who was to become my second wife. She had been a new friend of Ellie's, when she became a member of the Twentieth Century Club. My wife and her friends welcomed new members. Alice was a great asset with her family's connections to important lecturers and knowledge of fund-raising. I had already begun practicing medicine at Buffalo General Hospital, performing surgeries, but was not really involved with patient care. It felt empty. I transferred to the first hospital established in Buffalo, Sisters' of Charity, and there I found that working as a teaching surgeon, was much more rewarding.

I was quite happy for a number of years, and so was Ellie. She was very involved with fund-raising, organizing different events, and keeping the other ladies of Buffalo society busy, doing good things for Buffalo.

We resided in a modest home across from Delaware Park, enjoying the Art Gallery, its concerts, walks to restaurants on Elmwood, and attending theater, lectures; so many other pleasant activities. But, I'm avoiding the true theme of this story and am wandering into reminiscences. Forgive me. Back to Alice's dinner parties after Ellie's passing.

It took a while, but my resistance to Ellie's friends trying to get me to re-join life was fading. I was ready to move on.

Ellie's friends encouraged me to date Alice Wicks. They meant for me to get to know this wonderful woman who could help me out of my grief. They convinced me that forming a new friendship would make Ellie happy.

Alice's home on Jewett Parkway was enormous, and she had an independent income from her parents' trust fund. She also had a son, who was thirteen. The same age as my son, Charles,…Charlie. Her son….is Jackson.

I mentioned details about my early career, because that's how Alice Wicks got me interested in her. She was sponsoring a few student nurses at Sisters' who couldn't afford the tuition but who were interested in careers in nursing. She invited me to a dinner party she was hosting as a benefit to raise more scholarship money for the nursing students. I was happy to attend.

This new friendship went smoothly. I was surprised that my grief lessened with each of our meetings. We became known as a *couple* within our circle of friends. It was a natural way to move on. My son, Charley, was glad that his old Dad had found a loving companion. He seemed to get along fine with Jackson…at the beginning.

I learned later, at subsequent dinners, and outings, that Jackson, was abandoned by his father, when the divorce was settled. Her first husband was a philandering gambler, who had married Alice for her trust fund. She told me she had been blind, incredibly naïve, and sheltered from such people because of her wealthy background. She had attended Buffalo Seminary and was accustomed to people with money. She had thought everyone had fortunes."

I could relate, as I had thought the same thing, growing up in affluence. I used to even blame the poor, themselves, for being stuck in poverty."

Justin continued, "Of course, wealth doesn't guarantee that handsomeness, charm or beauty is also a birth-right, so she was smitten by a riding instructor at the Delaware Park Stables where she was taking riding lessons. She knew he had no money. Instead, he made her laugh, was incredibly handsome, virile, and irresistible. When her parents inquired as to what his family background was, she rebelled and said it didn't matter. She was in love with him and there was no one else in their stodgy old circle of friends that attracted her and that she would end up being a spinster and they would have no grand-children from her.

They relented, with objection, and a beautiful society wedding was held at the Statler Hilton Ballroom, complete with horse-drawn carriages and 12 bridal attendants. She showed me a clipping form the *Courier-Express* that included a huge spread of the lovely bride and her handsome groom. It even made the Society Section of *The New York Times* and *Town and Country* Magazine."

During his story, my mind was trying to absorb the picture he was painting. Nothing indicated, yet, why Jackson caused so much animosity. Justin didn't seem the type to judge people harshly, without just cause.

Martin had heard this story before, but had the courtesy to remain silent and hear it all again.

We each had refills of out honey brandy. It relaxed us, and brought such comforting warmth, I hoped I wouldn't dose off if Jackson's story became too drawn out. I needn't have worried. The remaining parts kept me wide awake. It shocked me to understand that Jackson was worse than I had thought in lacking morals and human decency. People like him do not believe they ever do anything wrong.

Justin continued, "Unfortunately, Alice's fairy-book story wedding kind of turned out like Princess Margaret's. who had fallen in love with a photographer, a commoner who had numerous extra-marital affairs, causing Britain's Royals much scandal. Their union ended in divorce. It didn't work out for Alice, either. She quickly learned that her new husband was fond of horses in a betting way. He rode them, but they almost rode the couple into bankruptcy. Many arguments later, she found out she was pregnant. Her parents were to have a grand-child, but they no longer needed the son-in-law. A quick divorce was granted, and the soon-to-be father was banished with a large sum of money to some place in Florida, with the mandate he was never to be seen in Buffalo again, and he must give up all paternal rights, or else his trust fund would be terminated.

Alice was more relieved than heart-broken. She was embarrassed that she had been so completely duped, and was determined to raise her child as a single mother with the help of her parents. Her father knew some real estate brokers who enabled her to live in the house on Jewett with the attending nannies, tutors, maids, and cooks.

Mind you, Alice was not spoiled. She thought most people had these luxuries and was a very generous loving woman, in spite of all she was born with. She was lovely, charming, wealthy, intelligent, and I would have been crazy not to ask her to share the rest of her life with me. We were both in our 50's, single, with sons.

Ellie and I had had trouble getting pregnant, so we didn't have more children, other than Charlie. He was 15, when Alice and I married."

# Chapter 31

I had thought this sad story was over. There was enough tragedy. But Martin urged Justin to complete it. He did:

"I was lucky to have met Alice and married her. Unfortunately, Jackson, her son was very spoiled. He expected people to defer to him."

"Wait." I couldn't keep silent that long. "Isn't *Jackson* a family name?"

"Ironic that he has the same initials as myself and my father, isn't it? What's not ironic is that Jackson also believed that my son, Charley, was in the way of his getting everything his little heart desired.

I was away at the hospital, long hours at a time, so I didn't see the animosity building between my son, and my step-son, Jackson. My wife, Alice did, but she kept it from me, hoping it was just a case of severe sibling rivalry. It was the Bible's Cain and Abel at our home. I even formally adopted him, hoping there would be a feeling of more equality between them."

"Where is your son, now?" I asked, anxious for a happy ending.

"One August morning, Alice took the boys to our summer home in Canada, a few miles from The Peace Bridge. Many Americans bought property along the Canadian shore back then, and kept the summer homes in their families from generation to generation.

Jackson wanted to go sailing. Alice said it was too rough on the river, and that he should wait for a calmer day. But he had acquired a new sailboat from his grandparents for his sixteenth birthday, and it was already moored, waiting to be used.

There was no way Jackson could ever accept a negative response to his requests. He's still that way.

Alice repeated her warning and refused to grant him permission. But, *No* was and still is not part of Jackson's vocabulary. He told Charley that he had permission to go out on the boat, as long as Charley went with him. Charley was a stronger swimmer than Jackson, and had even worked as a life guard at the summer camp for disadvantaged children in Angola."

Justin paused, and poured each of us a bit more brandy to distract us from the tears welling up in his eyes.

"Forgive me, I haven't told this part out loud, ever, except to Martin. I'm still surprised by my emotional reaction.

Anyway, this story ends with Jackson and Charley sailing out on the rough waters. The wind was kicking up and suddenly a strong gust caught the sail and swung the mast around, hitting Charley in the head, knocking him unconscious, causing him to fall over-board. The strong Niagara current swept him along down river. Jackson could do nothing but watch my son disappear below the swells."

I felt a sudden pall fall over our heads. I knew there would be no happy ending.

"If this is too difficult for you Justin, you don't have to continue."

Justin looked at Martin for support. Martin nodded, encouraging the doctor to continue. I hoped all the grief would finally spill out and give Justin the healing he was still in such need of.

Many times, when people in emotional pain can finally talk about things, the pain subsides, leaving scars, of course, but releasing the choke hold it has on the heart.

"If I don't continue, my grief may never be healed. You're the spiritual healer. I can only help bodies. I told you, you have an open face, mind, and heart. Let me show you my wound, and maybe you can help heal it.

When I told this story to Martin, I was able to at least look at it, logically. But reason has nothing to do with the heart. I still feel like the past has eaten up so much of my present. Now that my future is being counted in hours, I would like to meet my Maker, free of all this anguish, hurt, and even hate. If I hadn't held Jackson and his mother responsible for all my grief, maybe Jackson wouldn't have turned out to be the man I can't stand to look at in the present."

We were all silent, taking in the emotional impact of this story of family sadness. Sometimes the best response is silence. Words can be more harmful than respectful silence in the presence of extreme emotional distress.

But as a spiritual healer, I was obligated to offer some words of consolation. I prayed they would be the right ones, inspired by the Holy Spirit.

Taking a deep breath, I tried my best.

"Justin," I began gently, "we are all responsible for our own actions. You are taking responsibility now for your feelings. But Jackson still has to learn that his actions have consequences, as well.

You told me about Mandy and how his relationship with her caused her so much pain. Lexie, Mandy's own sister will be hurt, because of this situation, even if it occurred in the past. I'm sure his ex-wife could blame him for much misery he must have caused her. Now he wants to be a public servant! Do you see how impossible it will be for him to give of himself for the public's good, when he can't even do it in his personal life?"

After sighing deeply, Justin continued with relating the rest of his personal tragedy:

"Alice learned that the boys had gone out on the sailboat and asked our neighbor to take his motorboat out to haul them back in. The neighbor returned, towing the sailboat. Only Jackson was aboard. He told his mother about the accident and that Charley had fallen into the water and had probably made it to shore, and was most likely waiting for them to pick him up about three miles down-river.

The Coast Guard was called, and Charley was found. Only it was his unconscious body that had made it to shore, a few miles down, caught up on some rocks. He was able to live with a ventilator, while I called in the best doctors I knew for advice and a miracle. But his brain had suffered too much trauma from lack of oxygen. I was grateful that he was given back to us for a bit, and that he wasn't found on the Lower Niagara after going over the Falls.

His organs weren't even saved, as transplantation was just in its pioneer stages. It seems, my life as a doctor, healing others, took me away too much from my loved ones, so that I don't even have sufficient memories to sustain me on lonely nights."

The doctor's emotional suffering was palpable. In sharing his tragedy, his psychic pain could become more bearable. In grief counseling, people are encouraged to breakdown and share. The pain is dispersed. It hurts, but doesn't fester inside, causing depression and bitterness. Eventually, the talking part ebbs, as acceptance of the tragedy becomes more apparent. People who cannot share their human emotional pain can become isolated and even suicidal. It's important for every listener to understand that just listening is the best they can do for those in anguish.

"I'm sure when such tragic accidents occur," I tried to explain, "there's enough blame to go around to everyone. Even God is blamed, and fate, karma, but for some reason, never randomness. I don't believe bad things happen to punish anyone. I do believe they are difficult to accept, let alone explain. There is no logical explanation, when such horrible things happen, without provocation, as in pre-meditated murder. As humans, we have difficulty accepting the frailty of life. Every day is a miracle that we survive. Sorry, I didn't mean to sermonize. Know that I acknowledge the immensity of your pain. That kind never goes away. It ebbs and flows like a great ocean of sorrow."

"Thank you, friends, for allowing me to wallow in my misery. Martin has heard this story too many times. I needed to say it out loud to you, Rob, as a kind of confession as to why I hate Jackson. I don't really hate him anymore, though. I guess it's worse. I have no feelings for him anymore. It's deepened into indifferent contempt.

In order to cope and continue with some kind of worthwhile life, I gave up hospital work and began a private practice. Jackson never apologized for disobeying his mother. He didn't shed one single tear of remorse. Alice was devastated by the accident, but never blamed her son for his disobedience or held him the least bit accountable.

The poor woman coped by drinking too much. I was completely shut down, emotionally. Passive-aggressiveness can hurt the person it's directed toward as much as physical abuse.

One night, after drinking heavily, she looked at me, sitting sullenly in front of the TV, took the car keys, and hit a tree, head-on. She died, instantly."

Martin had not said a word while Justin poured out his anguish. I was waiting for some angel to whisper the healing words in my ear that Justin needed to hear, but the silence in that room was deafening.

Finally, Martin was the one who offered the first emotional band-aid. "Justin, you must know that Jackson was and is mostly concerned with his own being. For whatever reason, he is concerned primarily with only his needs. He looks at people as objects that will help him get what he wants. The women who have tried to change him through love, care, and giving in to his every desire have been disappointed and left by the way-side. Poor Lexie is his next victim.

I know if Mandy told her to watch out for her soon-to-be-husband, her sister would cut her off completely from her life. You and I have already discussed Jackson's interest in making Lexie his wife. She is certainly beautiful and intelligent. But her background has no connections to wealth that Jackson could use. His first wife, at least had family connections that helped him attain his status in City Hall."

"Do you know why they split?" I asked, trying not to change the direction of Martin's attempt to help Justin's emotional pain, but I couldn't help myself.

Justin said, "It's another long story that also proves how Jackson uses people without any pangs of conscience."

"Sorry, Martin. Please go on with what you and Justin concluded about Jackson's interest in Justin's nurse, Lexie."

"We couldn't come up with a definite reason. We can only assume that her being Justin's nurse and having such free rein in his private apartment here, can only benefit him somehow."

"Isn't he afraid Mandy might reveal his true nature to her sister?" I found Jackson to be highly repugnant. Obviously, he's able to change his persona when forming relationships with women. As an armchair psychologist, I can deduce that he might even detest men because of his own biological father's lack of character. He must have learned at an early age how to manipulate women like he did his own mother. He also must have heard nothing but negative reviews of his biological father. A very powerful potion in forming a young child's view of personal relationships.

"Remember," Justin said, "even Jackson doesn't know about Mandy's pregnancy. Revealing that now would only make Lexie think that Mandy was jealous of her and was making up a story. Mandy works with Jackson, don't forget. Lexie might not be able to see how any woman wouldn't want her own chance at landing Jackson for herself."

Once again, the green-eyed monster can make people blind to the truth. Jealousy truly is one of the Deadly Sins.

"This is going in so many different directions, it's too late to try and untangle each facet." I knew some space and rest would help each of us think more clearly. "I have this week-end tied up with festive obligations. Now that's an oxymoron, I know, but since we've agreed to meet next Thursday, let's call it a night and see if we can digest these details by ourselves, then meet with fresh perspectives. Maybe we'll be able to figure out a way to save Lexie from Jackson, as well as the public from his venture onto the political stage."

"Sounds like a plan, Rob." Martin stated. "I can follow you home. It's dark and your neighborhood isn't the safest this time of night."

Justin saw us out and bid us Good-night. He was exhausted, but seemed much more at peace. His courage in going over his past, was medicine for his soul.

"It's only 9 o'clock, Martin. It's not the Middle East of the Arab world. It's the east side of Buffalo."

"Suit yourself. But let me know if you'll be needing a doctor. Justin's off-duty, but I'm sure he'd come to assist if a friend's been mugged."

I assured him I'd be fine and told him of my frequent walks down the dark streets when an urge for Norm's pizza beckoned.

"Alright then. I'll be at your big party on Saturday at the Grand Central Terminal, of all places. Isn't that a bit over-the-top for you?"

"Martin, my girls think only the best is good enough for me, their favorite bachelor. Plus, they think I have first-class VIP passes to heaven."

"See, you next Thursday, then," Justin said. "Partying is no longer on my bucket list, though I hope a good time will be had by all, this Saturday."

He assured us he was fine.

"I may be a bit brandied out, but telling you my story has brought me some comfort. I know things happen for a reason. But when they happen to people one loves, that saying is meaningless. Time can bring perspective. I still don't understand the why of it. It frustrates me. We'll have to discuss all this at our next meeting, Rob. Think about what you can say to me that will help me accept this, and bring me to an even better place."

Martin and I parted ways outside. He was a good man. Thank God, I gave him a chance to show me his true nature. When we first met, I had been put off with his intrusion into my past.

It was good to know I could still make friends, especially with people who are familiar with the era I am in and from. Martin and Justin are just the friends I need to help me understand the new directions life is taking the younger generations. We can debate, discuss, and offer new perspectives to each other, from masculine points of view.

My girls are wonderful. But every man needs a group of friends he can simply be a man around, without worrying about offending lady-like sensibilities. Sometimes I even stifle a yawn, for fear of it being taken the wrong way by one of the girls. Heaven forbid a hearty burp, or an escape of gas.

*Ahhh. This is going to be nice.* I can even talk about my love of Westerns with my male counterparts I know they'll be able to relate.

# Chapter 32

Driving home along the 33, I was again grateful that Buffalo was so easy to get around in, except for the new areas being developed along the Outer Harbor. That was once the neighborhood of ill-repute, when freighters pulled in with their grain, steel, lumber, and produce. Bars and loose women lined the canal, as well as thieves, murderers, and loan sharks. My neighborhood was tame by comparison, except for the few gangs that claimed it as their territory. They knew who I was and they knew the Mission helped their mothers, younger siblings and girlfriends who bore their children, while they played gangsters.

I was trying to reach out to the gang members, one at a time, like Antoine and Marcus. Hopefully, they'll make it in school this time and see that hard work pays off. The problem is the easy work on the street paid better in cold cash. Their only danger was finding themselves at the end of cold gun barrels, if they were lured back.

I was soon pulling into Lenore's parking space, that was well-lit with cameras all over the place for added protection. Martin needn't have worried. I've been able to take care of myself all these years. I was more afraid of having to face all the well-wishers at my party on Saturday than some person on the street asking for a hand-out.

There was some paper work I needed to finish up in my office. One quality I was happy to possess was that I was not a procrastinator. Getting things done in a timely manner was important to me. Lenore had even told me that this quality alone would have made me a great husband. Tina had agreed, adding that appreciation for home-cooking was another husbandly attribute.

The door to the rectory was locked. I had some trouble fitting in the key. It seemed to be warped or something. I'd have to talk to one of the grounds-keepers tomorrow. I'd be getting up early, anyway to prepare for Mass. Lenore's last chance to bring me the plans for re-doing the rectory might have to wait till next week, if she doesn't drop by tomorrow.

I was grateful my old-fashioned black desk telephone wasn't attached to an answering machine. What did people do to communicate before the invention of the phone?

I had to check on the notes I'd left for myself on my desktop to make sure tomorrow's schedule would be planted in my brain. I knew there were a few things I needed to take care of before the weekend officially began. At least, I thought I'd left the notes on my desk.

I began opening my drawers to see if I had buried them. *What in the name of...was this*? There was a gallon-size baggie full of some kind of pills! They weren't mine, that's for sure. Someone must have left them there, or planted them ...but why?

My mind was trying to slow down and explain all this...when...

"Father Rob? Sorry to have come so late. The rectory door was unlocked, so I just walked in."

"Sorry if I'm in a daze. I just found something in my desk drawer and I'm trying to understand why it's there. I've had some lapses of memory, lately."

"Here, let me have a look. Maybe I can help."

Part Two

# Chapter 33

"Dammit, Rob! This isn't the day for you to over-sleep."

Lenore was trying to call Rob on the phone, and getting nowhere.

"*Lucky for you, I'm just across the courtyard.*" Lenore often talked out loud to herself when she was stressed.

She had the rectory re-modeling plans for Rob to look over, but needed to attend to a million other things. Rob's 50thh year Anniversary party was tomorrow. Shelly and Tina would be over in half an hour to finalize the plans.

Grabbing her design book, she glanced at the materials she had chosen to give the rectory the polish it needed to be seriously comfortable. Deep leather chairs in burgundy would complement a beautiful teak-wood main desk. There would be an over-head lighting fixture of brass that was subtle enough not to compete with the brass desk lamp with the beautiful pleated burgundy shade.

She also noted the growing cobwebs, and decided it was time to hire a weekly cleaning crew. It had been a while since she had inspected this building where Rob had his office.

The oak wainscoting would remain intact, but the walls would have a dark green wallpaper with burgundy and gold subtle striping. New oak built-in book shelves with file drawers would replace the beat-up old metal filing cabinets. The oak floors would be re-finished and a silk antique Persian rug she had saved from one of her other re-modeling ventures would suit the rectory more than the modern, chrome-themed condo she had decorated last year.

She was extremely pleased with her efforts, and hoped Rob would be too. He was easy to please though. Her toughest job would be to convince him to replace his old black desk phone with a modern answering system, that could record messages and even take dictation for transcription to a printer. That would definitely be her challenge today, but she was up for it.

She always enjoyed taking an old, worn-out room and transforming it into a place of serene, subtle beauty, that captured the essence of the person who would be spending the most time in it. Her twin brother, Jaime did this for his patients. He was a plastic surgeon in England. It was a shame he couldn't cross the pond for tomorrow's celebration. Rob had also saved him from poverty when they were both so young and parent-less.

So many people had been helped by this priest she considered her own personal guardian angel. She knew the Memorial would resound with grateful people from all walks of life and all ages.

It astounded her every time she realized Rob could relate to the souls of people. He rarely, if ever, commented on their physical appearances. That's probably the reason why he never complained about the rectory being in dire need of a make-over. Luckily, he had women friends who noticed these things.

The door to the rectory was open. She was glad that Rob was up, even though he had probably missed saying Mass. His parishioners knew that if he wasn't hearing confessions before Mass, he most likely was called away and would not be celebrating it that day. They understood and did not wait for his appearance. They basically said a rosary or their daily prayers, instead. The shortage of priests made these inconveniences happen.

The lack of vocations for the priesthood and the sisterhood was staggering. The Church would have to come up with a solution to this American dilemma. Churches all over the world, didn't seem to have this problem. This was a discussion for another day. Today she was the designer, eager to show her plans to Rob, for his approval. If all went well, the transformation could begin next week.

"Oh, Rob...I'm here to show you the magic I've dreamed up to make your life more beautiful in this old rectory."

She was walking through the entry hall, making mental notes of how to re-furbish its tired appearance as well.

At the doorway to the office, she began to scold.

"Don't tell me you're still sleeping? Missing Mass isn't enough? Now you want to sleep away the morning?"

She approached the desk, where Rob had his head down, resting on his arms.

"Rob? Are you awake? Are you fooling around?"
She realized that he was not going to wake up.

"ROB!!!" She dropped her plans and quickly dialed 911 on the old black phone. There was no dial tone. It was dead.

Her cell was deep in her briefcase. With trembling hands, she retrieved it and was able to call for immediate help.

There was no way she could move from the floor. She dared not touch anything, but also called the police. She was alert enough and called Detective Foster, as his number was on her cell, thank God.

"Detective Martin? Please come to the Mission rectory as soon as possible. Something's happened to Rob."

The sirens were already getting closer, when Lenore was able to crawl over to the doorway. The EMTs came through the door, helping her up, while appraising the situation.

"I think it's too late," Lenore moaned.

A first responder confirmed that it was true. No pulse, no physical sign of life.

Two police officers entered the room.

"Appears to be a suicide," the EMT told the police.

"WHAT?" Lenore screamed. "No frickin' way!"

Detective Foster was at her side as she broke down into sobs.

"Looks like the bullet entered the base of the skull," the police inspector said. There are opiates scattered in this opened desk drawer."

"We'll have to close off this building to bring in the CSI's."

"Lenore, come with me out into the hall," Martin gently ordered.

"No. I need to stay with him. He didn't kill himself. No one will ever believe he did this to himself. Something else is going on. Don't you dare declare this a suicide, Inspector!"

"This is what my first assumption is, Ma'am. I'm sure you are highly distressed. Let us do our job, to find out what really happened here."

Lenore allowed Martin to lead her outside. Shelly and Tina came running up the walk. They were there to discuss the plans for the celebration, but immediately knew something had happened when they arrived. The ambulance, police cars, Lenore's sobbing made their adrenaline begin rushing through their bodies in torrents.

"It's Rob. He's gone!" Lenore clutched them into her arms. They swayed, and sobbed in unison.

# Chapter 34

Sitting in Lenore's office at the mission, the three women looked at each other in disbelief. Lenore's husband, Harris, brought them each a stiff shot of liquor. They sipped the strong elixir, feeling its warmth course through their shocked bodies.

"I know you want me to explain," Lenore began, "But all I can tell you is I walked over to the rectory and found him there, with his head down over his arms as if he was resting. When I approached, I knew instantly, that he wasn't there anymore and called 911, the police, and Detective Foster."

"I heard the word *suicide*," Shelly murmured. "Could it be?"

"No way," Tina was adamant. "He didn't want us to throw him a party, but he wasn't suicidal about it."

Her comment brought smiles to Lenore and Shelly. They nodded in agreement as they clasped hands.

The Inspector entered, and saw the women needed a report.

"There's a gun under his arms. It's been fired. It was most likely placed there to make us believe the Reverend had taken his own life.

The pills in his desk drawer are obviously a plant, to make us believe he was an addict. The front door lock was also tampered with, and we're dusting for prints now. I know Father Sullivan was a beloved figure in the community, but do you know if he had any enemies at all?"

"So, you believe it definitely was not suicide?" Lenore asked.

"As of now, we're calling it a homicide."

"This is just as horrible," Tina said. "But, if he had killed himself, it would have completely destroyed us. If we were completely unaware of his depression, we could never forgive ourselves."

"He was hiding something, though," Shelly admitted. "He's been quiet these last few days. I thought it was his reluctance to accept being the guest of honor at the party, but something else may have been bothering him."

"He did have a lot on his mind," the detective said. "After the official report is in, I'll try to clear all that up."

"Is it something we should know about now?" Lenore asked.

"It can wait. I'm afraid you have to use your energies right now, calling all the people expected at the anniversary tomorrow."

The women looked at each other, intently. They could read each other's minds. Lenore was the first to acknowledge what they were thinking.

"He got his wish about not being at this party we're throwing for him. But that doesn't mean he can't be there in spirit."

"That's right," Tina agreed. "We'll have the party tomorrow, in his honor, but it'll be not only a tribute to his life, but a memorial to honor his…." She couldn't say the word.

"His death," Shelly completed the thought. "We know this is difficult. We know he should still be here in body. But we also know his spirit is still with us. I can feel it. Can you guys?"

At that moment, a reporter from one of the local TV stations, then from *The News* appeared in the doorway.

"Sorry to barge in like this," the tiny woman reporter who looked about 12, to the women, gently began. "I can help broadcast a public statement on the afternoon and evening news channel, if you wish, about tomorrow's cancellation of events."

"There won't be a cancellation," Lenore sadly smiled. "The celebration will go on, without the bodily presence of the guest of honor."

"Off the record," Detective Foster said, "what better way to have so many suspects gathered in one place at the same time?"

"So, it's a homicide, not a suicide?" asked the male newspaper reporter. He looked a bit older; perhaps all of 13.

"Who did you hear it was a suicide from?" Tina asked defensively.

'We have police scanners, Ma'am. But we also received an anonymous call from someone confirming the death of Father Robert Sullivan, this morning."

"What time was that call received?" Martin Foster asked.

"Not sure of the exact time, sir. I was told by my editor to hustle down here. It took me about 15 minutes."

"Same thing happened to me." the young woman TV reporter announced. "The manager told me to get over here with a camera crew."

"Where are they now?" Martin asked.

"Shooting video of the Mission and its grounds. We couldn't get into the rectory itself. Still a crime scene."

"Can you give us a statement?" The reporter looked at Lenore. She knew the mission was her territory.

"For now, all I can say is that there is an active investigation occurring. Suicide has been explicitly ruled out. Also, the anniversary party planned for tomorrow at the Central Terminal will still be held. The starting time is different, though. It will begin at 4:00 PM. The people who knew Father Rob as a friend, will be asked to arrive at 3:00PM, for a private discussion and prayer."

"May we attend?" Both reporters asked in unison.

"Please respect our wishes, in that you will be welcome to attend at the public time of 4:00PM. Unless, there is a reason why you would need to attend the private gathering."

Lenore waited in the silence, then asked to be excused. Harris escorted the reporters out. He returned to see if there was anything else he could do, at the moment, for any of the ladies. He also agreed with them that the celebration should go on.

"There is not one reason to deny Father Rob's friends the privilege of saying good-bye to him in a public way. Whoever is responsible for this crime will be in attendance. I can assure you that such a heinous act will demand that the perpetrator be there to witness his or her success. Absence would cry out suspicion."

"But what if it was a gang member who wanted revenge for Rob taking away potential recruits?" Tina asked.

"In that case, I think if they do attend, it will be to gloat, and this will point out their guilt, as well."

The women put their hearts and heads together to compose a public statement for the press. Detective Foster approved it:

*"Some time, presumably last evening, our dear friend, Father Robert Sullivan was taken from us in an act of violence. This was not a self-inflicted act, as may have previously been reported. If you have been invited to Father Rob's Golden Anniversary Party tomorrow, please be aware that the public is still invited, to pay their respects. The Grand Central Terminal will be open to the public at 4:00 PM. If the spirit moves you, contributions for the restoration and preservation of the Terminal will be collected. This had been the plan for Father Rob's celebration. He would not have attended his own party, if this had not already been planned. Those of you who knew him, would agree that his own self-aggrandizement was non-existent. I am sure the person or persons responsible for this heinous act have already been forgiven by Father Rob's generous, compassionate spirit. That doesn't mean, however, that those responsible will not be brought to justice by those of us who lack this humble priest's magnanimous character. Thank you."*

"Well said," a familiar voice spoke from the doorway. The women rushed to embrace Nicki who had arrived from Canada, in time to hear Lenore read the press release.

The women held on to each other and sobbed.

Detective Foster felt confident that his new friend's murder would be solved. These women were strong, smart, and familiar with all Rob's friends and acquaintances. No one could escape their scrutiny. He would tell them the truths the priest had just recently learned, himself, about his true parentage. This would help explain to the four women why the priest seemed distracted. This would erase some of the guilt they felt in not recognizing signs before this tragedy.

## Chapter 35

### Lenore

Harris had already gone to bed. She had answered all the calls she possibly could, and finally sent out a text:

*Thank you for your concerns. We are all in deep shock. Tomorrow will be a sad day, but we will celebrate, along with mourn in grief. Father Sullivan would not like this much attention, but he will not be here to feel embarrassed. Hopefully, he will still be here with us in spirit to give us strength to see this through.*

She didn't have the strength this evening to write out some notes for the public memorial. She thought how ironic it was that the Central Terminal's address was Memorial Drive. She was drained...of tears, and logic.

"Hey. Do you want me to stay up with you, darling?" Harris knew his wife was exhausted, but asking her to sleep was out of the question.

"Just hold me Harris. We'll go to bed. Your arms will comfort me."

Harris guided his fragile wife to the safe haven of their bed, knowing that now, she needed human warmth more than words or anything else in the cold world that took away one of her dearest friends. Lenore would not be the same person if Rob hadn't agreed to help her grandmother find a foster-family for her and her twin, Jaime, so many years ago, when her parents had died. He was grateful to Rob, also, for all his support, physical, emotional, and financial, that allowed the mission to flourish in one of the toughest neighborhoods of the city. He knew someone had planned this murder with a great deal of thought, but also someone who had access to a gun and opioids. The mystery was why someone needed to make this priest go away, forever.

## Shelly

Rob Sullivan was the love of her life, right after her true love, Scott, had passed away, too soon. Tina had introduced her to him, shortly after moving back to Buffalo from South Carolina. They had been friends at college, and picked up their friendship, immediately.

Shelly remembered how being in Father Rob's presence had comforted her. He had encouraged her to continue her work of trying to preserve the precious buildings in the city and its surroundings that were a living museum of Buffalo's past and also a key to its future prosperity.

He was always generous with his time and donations at her fund-raising events.

*"Sometimes, we Americans can act like barbarians, Shelly," he admitted. "We let ourselves be hood-winked into believing developers are the saviors of a city's progress. They promise jobs in constructing new buildings. But there are also jobs in restoring and preserving that last far longer than a quick construction project. So many politicians are in the pockets of these developers, they say yes to every project, whether it makes sense or not. I enjoy our modern downtown library, but the old one that was destroyed is still a travesty. Interiors can be modernized, like our beautiful old post office building. on Ellicott. Its Gothic style designed by James Knox Taylor is a tribute to the artistry of architects. Architecture isn't merely for function. It has the power to elevate man's spirit. That's why so many cathedrals were successfully erected on the backs of the poor. Our churches were built by the poor immigrants who recognized the importance of buildings."*

Rob's encouragement gave her the will to keep living in spite of her desire to sell her Queen Anne that she and Scott had lovingly restored, when she had been determined to wither away in her small apartment on Elmwood. Selling the Queen Anne would have put all those lovely memories with Scott into the grave with him. She wasn't aware that she was actively doing this.

Rob was gentle in reminding her that her love for Scott was not replaceable.

Whenever she stayed at the Queen Anne, usually to host a tea or have her nieces sleep over, the immense happiness she felt was a comfort. It was a blessing she had not sold it. It might already have been torn down to accommodate more apartment buildings. She was grateful for her friends and grateful Rob had never made her feel humiliated when she had tried a few times to seduce him.

*"I know you have so much love in you, Shelly. You don't know what to do with its over-flowing quantity, now that Scott isn't here to absorb it."* He had reminded her that she still had nieces, a sister, and a brother-in-law, not to mention, dear friends who needed her. He hadn't try to make her feel guilty or ashamed about her trying to replace Scott with her infatuation with him. Many widows must have attempted the same thing. She was able to get his message, thank God, without it going further than a few erotic dreams.

She was spared humiliation and realized his friendship and guidance was much more worthwhile than a physical romantic tryst. It must have been a relief to him when he saw that she had ceased in her pursuit of him. She smiled recalling when this understanding became apparent.

She had been calling him, asking him to come out to dinner with her, in order to advise her in her grief. He never refused, but also never accepted her invitation to come to her apartment for after-dinner coffee. A theme of their dinners was often repeated when she began complaining to him about the Church's rule on celibacy for priests.

"It's really archaic, Rob. I mean there is no modern religious group that doesn't allow its ministers to marry. Don't you think this is causing all the pedophilia scandals?"

He had stopped eating, with a fork mid-air full of pasta, ready to be devoured. She knew this meant he was going to say something serious.

She also knew he had seen through her clumsy attempts to get him to admit that celibacy was wrong. Instead, she was relieved when he tactfully, set her straight.

*"Shelly, no matter what the Church's official ruling is, I choose to be celibate. I could never devout my entire being to my congregation, if I had complicated family dynamics to deal with. Families and their intricacies are complex. I would never be able to deal with infants, teenagers, spousal needs, and still have the energy to deal with those of other families.*

*Pedophilia is not confined to priestly abuse. Unfortunately, the priests guilty of this will have to answer for their sins more publicly that those who are guilty of it in a more private sector. Sin is reprehensible because it usually involves all of humanity. One sin has ripple effects, just as one good act of virtue does. That's why confession is so necessary. Jesus died so our sins might be forgiven, if we are in remorse and atone. There is no way to stop people from sinning. There is no way to stop people from practicing goodness. It boils down to choices, personal responsibility, and conscience-driven."*

Her conscience immediately responded to his words, and she decided that her attempt to seduce this good priest was not in her, his, or anyone's benefit. She would not listen to her selfish need to love and be loved. She did not ask him to return to her apartment that evening. She did, however, make a suggestion that they get together with Tina and Lenore next time, to enjoy a meal with other good friends.

He had smiled in response, and nodded saying, *"That's a great idea."*

## Tina

Tina could not stop staring out at the lake when she returned to her loft. The water was calm; her thoughts were like high waves breaking over her mind. She almost felt sea-sick. What had just happened? Who would she ever cook for again? There was no one who appreciated her culinary efforts more than Rob. Any chef will tell you that, like other artists, the product can do no good if it's not appreciated by others.

Who in the world, their world, would try to rid it of such a good person? Her mind ping-ponged without any solid conclusions. Detective Foster had said that he would have a list of potential perpetrators tomorrow. But this was still tonight. There would be no sleep. Thank God, she was such an organized person. All the food preparations for the anniversary were ready. She knew Rob would approve. There was no doubt his spirit was still around them. He would never leave without some form of good-bye.

Nicki had arrived just in time. She was in shock, but when she calmed down after realizing what had occurred, she was able to re-assure all the women that Rob had not left, yet.

"Even though the after-life's doors are ready to accept him, I know he won't leave us until more clarity develops. I feel him and his love surrounding us."

"Are you sure? Tina timidly asked. She knew Rob believed in Nicki's psychic abilities, but she was still skeptical.

Nicki smiled, brightly. "Don't worry, Tina. There will be a sign. And, you'll know it when it comes."

Nicki had formed a prayer circle, then and there. When they had clasped hands, a feeling of complete joy enveloped them. They looked at each other and smiled. How could this be? They should all be horrified and joined in sadness. Nicki assured them that this was Rob's way of embracing them and communicating that everything would be fine, and that he was fine. Even happy, as a matter of fact.

Detective Foster was not a part of this group. He had left, but also had assured them that this would all be made right.

"Whoever set this up is not a professional. It looks like someone was coerced into making this look like a suicide. Obviously, the person or persons involved, may have been recognized by Rob, as there is no sign of struggle. There are enough clues to sort out for an answer. There is also a very short-list of prime suspects. This is not a crime of passion, hate, or revenge. I suspect there is more a motive of convenience."

He wouldn't elaborate more, but his confidence gave the women more reason to feel that this horrible act would not go unsolved.

Tina didn't know what she would say tomorrow. Her mind was still flashing memories of laughter shared, as well as tears.

Rob had helped her through some of the darkest days of her life…after the devastation of losing her daughter. Her grand-daughter, Tia had called her after hearing about the murder on the late evening news. She was on her way over to spend the night with her grandmother. The key in the lock, brought her mind into focus. Once again, she would have to appear strong, in order to spare Tia concern for her mental state. It didn't work.

As soon as Tia entered the living room, Tina ran to her, and embraced her in a torrent of tears. The child would have to comfort her grandmother. But Tia was a beautiful grown woman. She was able to give comfort now. She held Tina close, and allowed her to complete her break-down.

They sat on the beautiful sofa, Lenore had chosen to complement Tina's loft of comfort. It was a high nest of soft greens, golds, taupes, and crimsons. She had felt immense comfort living here with her grandmother, after her own parents had died, when she was a young teenager.

Tina allowed her grand-daughter to help her prepare for a few hours of sleep.

"I'm better, now, Tia. Thanks for helping me pick up my mental pieces. I was able to hold it together for most of the evening."

They took big sighs together, and smiled.

"Rob must have paid me a visit just now and brought me some peace of mind. I'll be fine now. Thank God for you, and my wonderful friends. We'll all meet up with Rob one day…and not too much longer now,"

"Gram! That's enough of this talk. You'll begin to make me cry."

"Sorry, Tia. I didn't mean to upset you, darling girl. I should realize that I'm not your age, even though I feel like it. One good thing is that all my dear friends will be meeting up with Rob in the near future. I'll have to be more accepting of the inevitable."

"Gram!!! Please!"

Tina and Tia then broke into laughter. Sometimes that is the best medicine.

## Nicki

"It was a shock, Detective Foster, I mean Martin. Thanks for keeping in touch with what you already know."

Nicki was staying at the Mission with her husband, Lowell. They were here in the States for the 50th Anniversary party, but were now part of the Memorial and also, now part of the investigation.

Of all the women close to Father Robert Sullivan, Nicki was the closest. He had saved her from drowning, back when she was a teenager. That experience had opened the door to the psychic world for her. Rob never doubted her abilities and even came to her for dream interpretations. He believed in the world of spirit.

They were so close, some people believed Rob would have left the priesthood for her. This wasn't the type of relationship they shared. They were still close, but Nicki had married Lowell and helped him run his family vineyard in Canada.

Martin asked her to help him make a list of potential enemies of the murdered priest. It was definitely determined to have been a homicide.

"I truly feel Rob was just as surprised by this act as all of us were. I can almost sense him laughing at the irony of it all."

Nicki was not able to coat her feelings with somberness despite her personal grief. She knew that the place Rob was now in was a holding center. He wouldn't leave them with questions and concerns.

Her complete faith in an after-life made her put aside her feelings of loss, and focus on the investigation at hand. Of course, she would miss him, but believed she would see him again in the not so distant future.

"I'll be happy to try and sense if the person responsible for Rob's death will be at the Memorial in the Central Terminal. The problem is, there will be hundreds of souls asking why, feeling anger, and even some who will be unable to think clearly at all. Picking out the one soul who is guilty, will be like picking out one grain of sand on a beach full. It's worth a try, though. I'll try my best. There could be a better outcome, if I'm allowed in the interrogation room with any suspects you may be able to come up with."

Foster agreed and said he might be able to make that possible.

He told Nicki that he had visited Dr. Daniels later, the night of the discovery. The doctor confirmed that Rob was not the least bit suicidal. Rob and he were visiting the doctor earlier as friends, listening to the good doctor pour out his own feelings.

"I think you should also know, Nicki, the bag of opioids in Rob's desk drawer may be a red herring, or may be something he acquired due to some pain getting older may have induced. What's your opinion?"

"They're not his, Martin. I believe they were planted there to act as a motive. Rob had problems with is family when he was younger, but he never complained about any physical ailments. The most he complained about was being hungry."

They both smiled, remembering how much Rob was attracted to things that appealed to his sense of taste.

"For a man of the cloth, he certainly had his physical senses well-developed. You don't think there's a spurned lover somewhere in this mess, wanting retribution?"

"I have to laugh at that assumption, Martin," Nicki was greatly amused. "Don't you think this type of motive may have been played out years ago, when everyone knows he has a posse of adoring women tending to his every need?...except in the sexual department, of course."

"I realize I was grasping, but I have to allow for every avenue of possibility if I'm to solve this case."

"I'm glad you are. Sometimes there are so many murders being committed lately, and so many drug over-doses, the regular police department can't possibly be on top of this situation."

"Let your friends know, Nicki, that I promise I will try to get to the bottom of this as soon as possible. Will you be speaking tomorrow, at the Memorial?"

"No. Lenore will be in charge of the eulogy. She's known him since she was a child. I've known him since I was teenager, but I need to rely on my inner strength to see if I can come up with some sense of who would be capable of such a tragic act. It must come from some sort of desperation."

"Or, as I believe, some kind of reason why someone felt the priest's presence was an inconvenience."

"Do you think it was a gang member?"

"I think that someone with more intelligence wants us to believe that. But gangs usually shoot, run, and don't bother planting fake evidence."

When Detective Foster left, Nicki settled into a meditative state to clear her thoughts, calm her mind, and feel any type of communication from Rob, himself.

She was rewarded. Within fifteen minutes in her self-hypnotic state, she felt her spirit rise and felt Rob's warmth embrace her.

*"I saved you, once...I know you'll be returning the favor. All will be revealed...then I will leave to meet up with you on the other side, when it's your time."*

Nicki felt the peaceful assurance that all would be well. She trusted the message Rob's spirit had sent her. She thanked God for His gift to her and went to help Lenore prepare for the next day's Memorial.

# Chapter 36

Martin wasted no time in his pursuit of the truth. He was not about to allow another case to remain unsolved before he met his maker. There were so many potential suspects, but he could think of no real motive. He knew that finding a motive usually led to a conviction. He also knew that this wasn't enough. Evidence had to be produced, or he would know who the perpetrator was, but the courts wouldn't convict without substantial evidence. This was no going to go the same way his failure to convict the murderers of Judith Lee Daniels.

He had let her down but her unsolved murder led him to make the acquaintance of Rob Sullivan, which ultimately led to a friendship. A friendship that was just developing. He admitted this is what caused him to feel Rob's death on a personal level. Being emotionally involved in a case could lead to mistakes in judgment. He was determined to be methodical. His interview with Justin Daniels had provided corroboration that Rob had not committed suicide. But, the pill situation intrigued him.

"Are you sure no one was given a large amount of pain pills from your office, Justin?"

"Quite sure, But, I don't keep an inventory that may be used against me by the authorities."

"How much do you trust that your nurse, Lexie hasn't been selling them on the side? She has a big wedding to pay for."

"I trust her, Martin. But I can't say for certain that she hasn't given some of the pills to her friends."

"Do you mind if I question her, after the Memorial?"

"Not at all. I'm sure you'll find that the pills I dispense aren't serious narcotics."

"What do you mean?"

"What time is the Memorial set for tomorrow?"

"Four o'clock. Are you planning on attending?"

"If I can get up. It's three o'clock in the morning now. You woke me up from a deep sleep, Martin. But, I'm glad you did. I'll try to sort things out in my old mind. Someone may be trying to frame me, as well, but I'm too old to matter or bother with being murdered."

"I didn't want to alarm you, but I thought of that, too. Who would benefit from you being busted for opioid distribution, illegally?"

Both men were silent There was a chance that whoever could benefit from the doctor's arrest, would also benefit from Rob's demise.

Martin believed it could be a drug dealer whose business was impacted by the doctor's dispensing of basically free pills. Rob's knowledge of the situation could have put him in jeopardy. He forgot to question the doctor about the pills not being "serious narcotics."

There was no real personal connection between the people the doctor knew and those Rob dealt with. Even Justin's son, Jackson had met Rob only once or twice. Rob threatened, but did nothing to prevent Jackson from pursuing a political career.

The frustrating thing was Rob had no voice mail that could help clear up the list of people who may have called him the last few days. There were no recording devices in his confessional, of course.

Whoever did it, knew that there would be a cold trail to follow, even if the planning of the actual murder was faulty. No evidence…no crime.

He went home to his apartment on the West Side. He lived modestly in an upper flat that over-looked the Niagara River. He loved the view, even if the Thruway cut across his access to the water line, itself. Tomorrow he would attend his new friend's Memorial Service. He would survey the attendees. Then he would return to his flat, grab his fishing gear, and throw a line in the river, hoping to connect with something of substance he may have over-looked in trying to come up with suspects.

Fishing always led to contemplation for him. Perhaps some real answers would also arise from his musings. Perhaps Nicki and he could put their minds together and come up with a plan to gather evidence. Evidence that would stick to the murderer and set Rob free.

## Chapter 37

The morning was cool, but sunny. Lenore had been able to fall asleep for about two hours. Harris had made sure her cell was on silent. He brought her a breakfast tray at 7:30 am.

"I must look like a banchee."

"I haven't heard you wail, darling, and you look nothing like a crazy person, out of control."

"Harris, thank you for the breakfast, but I think a slice of toast will do for now."

"How are you feeling? Emotionally."

"It's strange, but I feel good. Calm, in fact. It's as if Rob came to me while I was sleeping, and put his hand gently on my forehead, wiping away my anger."

"Anger?"

"I know. I don't feel sad as much as angry. How could he leave me...us,... so suddenly. I had felt it was his fault, somehow."

"It's part of the grieving process, Lenore. The intense sadness you feel for this loss is too much for your mind to handle, so it's displaced with anger, instead. Anger is a primitive emotion. Grief is something we poor mortals have that separates us from lower beings."

"That's not true, Harris. Animals feel loss. Elephants, especially, grieve for the death of their loved ones. Cats and dogs feel pain when their masters, die. I know for a fact, animals aren't lower beings. Why else would Noah be instructed to save them from the deluge?"

"Point taken, Lenore. Will you agree that certain people who cannot grieve, or are detached from feeling loss are mentally unhinged?"

"Yes. We call them psychopaths. But why are we even discussing all this?"

"Just trying to explain why you feel anger instead of being sad, my dear."

"I know, Harris. Sorry for being snippy. Must be lack of sleep. Coffee will improve my mood. Come here and let me feel your arms around me."

Lenore was an extremely busy woman. She ran her interior decorating business, the Mission, and also helped the refugees find their place in their new country. Her husband was the rock she was able to stay moored to during her emotional storms.

"Just promise me you won't leave me like Rob did. I pray to be the first to join him in Paradise."

"Behave yourself, then, so we can all be together in the great beyond."

Lenore hugged him tighter and felt herself relax in his arms. He always knew how to bring her back from the edge, by lightening up her heaviest concerns.

"I'm ready now, to face the day, Harris. No more fretting about the Memorial. You knew this is what was setting me up to be bitchy. I know what I'm going to say. Rob was feeding me an idea that will make this a truly memorable day."

Harris took her tone to mean she was planning something totally different from a sad eulogy. He was right.

# Chapter 38

By noon, the parking area around the Central Terminal was filling up. There were Mercedes, BMWs, Cadillacs, and other high end SUVs parked next to Pick-ups, mid-sized sedans, and motorcycles. The variety of vehicles showed Father Sullivan's far reach into all classes of people, regardless of their financial status.

Inside, Rob would have been extremely pleased by the smells of hot dogs grilling, polish sausage cooking, and the sounds of a polka band warming up. His girls had come through with everything they had promised.

Tina was pleased with the ambiance.

"This is what my friend would have wanted, Tia. He specifically asked for this menu of comfort food. I guess this will be more of a celebration of his life than we thought."

"I have to admit, Gram, I wasn't sure how this was going to work, but it does. I feel happy being here, actually."

Tina laughed. "So do I. Nicki told us Rob was still hanging around in spirit. It's strange but true. I feel him all around and can almost see him poking around, deciding which delicacy to have first. A hot dog or Polish sausage."

"Oh, No! Don't tell me that slime ball is attending? What could he possibly want besides campaigning at this event?"

Tia was referring to the appearance of Jackson Daniels.

"Rob had said he had met him, a little while ago. Maybe they had begun a friendship. Who's that with him?"

"That's his fiancé, Lexie. She works for his father as his nurse. If his ex-wife shows up, there might be fireworks at this Memorial, as well as carnival food."

"Let's hope he leaves before that happens, then."

"Too late. There she is coming through the entrance with a man."

"That man is Detective Foster, Tia. Come on, I'll introduce you, and hopefully the fireworks will fizzle."

Tina was surprised that Martin Foster was escorting such an attractive young woman. Her blond hair was cut in a modern de-constructed shag. She was as tall as a model, and wore a beautifully tailored black crepe one-piece jump-suit that was elegant and under-stated as a designer ensemble could be.

"Detective Foster…Martin, I'm glad you've arrived early," Tina said, knowing he was early enough to observe most of the guests entering through the main door.

"Good afternoon, Tina. This must be your granddaughter. The resemblance is obvious."

"Yes. Thankfully, Tia was able to attend. She's known Father Rob, since she was a child."

"This equally lovely lady at my side is my daughter, Merrill."

Tina smiled and shook her hand, as did Tia. Tina was surprised. For some reason, she had assumed that Martin was a bachelor.

"My wife passed away five years ago. Merrill accompanies me to many events like this for emotional support. Sometimes, she even allows one or both of her two children to come along to happier social events, like weddings."

"My father makes it sound like a chore," Merrill's smile was bright. She didn't seem like an angry scorned ex-wife.

"I see my ex-husband has already made his appearance. Poor Lexie. She doesn't know what she's in for."

Tina was not about to ask what Merrill meant by that statement. Tia didn't hesitate.

"I know what you mean, Merrill. Jackson and I were in college together. Luckily, I could see through his con artistry, especially when he found out I really didn't have any family money. All I had was love from my family."

Tina smiled, happy that Tia was with her at for emotional support, and that she still was an integral part of her in this life, even though they no longer shared the same living quarters. However, sometimes Tia told it like it is, too much. She hoped Merrill wasn't offended by this outburst.

"Sorry to say, I was charmed by him," laughed Merrill. It took me three years and two children later to finally see he married me for my mother's family money."

"My wife was born into one of Buffalo's most prominent families, Tina. I don't know what she saw in me, but we loved each other. I had met her, believe it or not, when I was moonlighting as a security guard at one of the expensive fund-raisers she was attending for some politician."

"I have my own trust fund, Merrill explained. Luckily for me and my two boys, Jackson wasn't able to get a nickel of it. That was my revenge for his many nights out cheating and conniving."

"Do you mind introducing Merrill to Lenore and Shelly? I think I just noticed Nicki getting some food at one of the stations. I want to check in with her."

"Certainly, Martin. Tia and I were on our way to the podium where Lenore is getting her notes ready for the eulogy."

It's so strange to feel so festive at a memorial service, Tia admitted. But it makes sense, knowing Father Rob's personality. Did you know him, Merrill?"

"Not on a personal level. But, I went to him for confession, many times. For a man who never married, he certainly had great insight into the problems marriages can be plagued with."

"That's why Lenore is perfect to give this eulogy. She practically lived with him at the Mission," Tina said. "He helped her throughout her life, as well as many others, including myself. I know she'll do a remarkable job of recalling and summarizing a life that was ended not necessarily too soon, but certainly not a necessary death by any means."

The Terminal was almost at capacity, when Lenore gave the signal she was ready to speak.

She looked around at the sea of faces. Some she knew well, some not at all. But all, or most of them had been touched by Rob in some way. It was so difficult to comprehend why someone would deliberately harm him, let alone kill him. But someone did.

In her heart, she believed Rob had already forgiven him or her and was probably joking about how he was only sorry about not being able to enjoy the feast of his favorite foods the girls had so lovingly prepared for his big bash.

It was with this thought in mind, she was able to begin her sincere eulogy with a smile:

## Chapter 39

*Welcome dear friends. Welcome to all who knew and loved Father Robert Sullivan. And welcome to all who knew of this amazing, humble, gentle, inspiring man. Father Rob's compassion went way beyond the limits of the Mission he helped to run. It went beyond the limits of Buffalo. It encompassed the refugees and forgotten souls who were struggling to survive in a world where wealth is power, but forgetful, at times, of those who need a helping hand to make it up a rung of the ladder to success*

Lenore looked at her close friends, who encouraged her to go on. She felt their support and knew she could complete the eulogy, though her heart, mind and soul were hoping to see Rob's face miraculous appear and tell them this was all a mistake, and he was still alive.

*Father Sullivan was born into a successful, wealthy family. Somehow, he was able to develop a social conscience that wouldn't allow him to be entrapped by the privileges of his birth. That's why, it is so unfortunate that someone thought his life was not worth living, and decided to end this wonderful gift of his being by trying to blemish it with innuendo and lies about drug addiction and suicide.*

Shocked gasps reverberated throughout the immense hall. No one had been prepared for this announcement.

The room began buzzing with comments. Many, present, had not heard of the violent nature of the priest's death, or the circumstances surrounding it. The news was very circumspect in its reporting. The only statement set forth was that the good priest had died, unexpectedly.

Martin and Nicki had agreed to station themselves at opposite sides of the vast reception space, to try to get some sense of who may not be acting appropriately, or perhaps was smirking, or even looked threatening.

Harris was also stationed away from Lenore so he could better survey the crowd, as were Tina, Shelly, Tia, and Nicki. Merrill was close by Tia's side. She was watching her ex-husband's demeanor. She knew he would be at an event where there was a large crowd to make his presence known and work it for election potential. She also knew there were a number of wealthy people here, who could be used for their donations and fund-raising efforts.

She had been gullible. There were many others who could be charmed by him as well.

"Look at all the reporters, Tia," Merrill said. "Jackson must be in his glory."

"I hope the newspapers focus on other people besides him, then. I can't stand ego-maniacs," Tia smiled in reply, happy that Merrill and she were on the same page.

Tia was charmed by Merrill's beauty, but also her candor about being fooled by her ex-husband. Her grandmother had nudged her to watch what she said, but she felt comfortable around Merrill, and was determined to get to know her better. It would be nice to have some younger friends around when she visited her grandmother. Even though she loved her grandmother's friends…they were from a different generation. It would be nice to have someone closer to her own age to relate to when she visited.

Reporters had surrounded Jackson. He had been busily answering their questions with a smile. When Jackson noticed Merrill, before Lenore's speech, he simply raised an eyebrow in greeting. She had offered back a look of disgust. There was no amount of charm he could possess that would ever make her think of him as anything but distasteful. It was surprising to her, though, that the young woman he intended on marrying, had no money or wealthy family to back him. She knew there must be something she had to offer besides her youth and beauty. Apparently, she came from a poor part of Buffalo. Perhaps that was her worth.

He was probably planning on using her background to further his election chances with that constituency. The incumbent would be difficult to defeat, as he had been in office for a decade. Buffalonians knew his name. They favored familiarity over progressiveness, as long as there was no scandal to turn them off.

Too bad she couldn't warn his fiancé before she made the mistake of marrying this handsome low-life. But there would be someone else, if not her. What was the use?

Her attention was drawn back to Lenore, as the crowd quieted down. Lenore looked beautiful, elegant, and confident. Her dark hair was pulled back into a top-knot. Her V-necked dress was crepe that draped gracefully along her slim figure. She was surveying the crowd before her, making eye-contact, commanding their undivided attention.

Then, in her deep, resonant voice, she continued her eulogy: No one could move. They were frozen in place. The knowledge that their priest had been murdered was beyond speculation about who may have committed it. They could only process the fact that murder had taken away their spiritual guide. They listened with their souls for guidance on what to do next.

*.   I realize most of you have just learned of the cause of Father Sullivan's untimely demise. I have just also been told that he may have been surprised by the attack, himself.*

*I've known him for many years, and he usually left the rectory door unlocked, even after being warned time and time again that people weren't as honest and trust-worthy as he seemed to believe.*

*Needless to say, I hope, and pray, that if anyone knows something or someone who can shed some light on this heinous act, the sooner you reveal your information, the sooner his loved ones and friends can find some peace. Today, right now, would be an excellent time to tell me, any of his friends, or Detective Foster what you may know*

*I've been told the longer a case takes to be solved, the less likely it will be. Let's not let this be our case. Someone must know something. Our cameras at the mission did not help us.*

*Let there be no doubt. Father Rob is not gone because he over-dosed, committed suicide, or died from natural causes. He was murdered.*

*Some desperate soul put a selfish need before considering all the lives that would be affected by the taking of this generous, loving, innocent life. Surely, if this person had a serious problem, he or she could have asked our priest for his help. That help would have been granted, immediately. Most of you, here, can attest to that.*

*But make no mistake, whoever is responsible will not find a minute of peace. We will find you. Such ugliness can never find a total hiding place. You will be brought into the light.*

Lenore paused, looking around the room. The sea of faces was silent. She had not expected so many. At least 800 people crowded into the Terminal. No one, of course, volunteered any information…yet. She had not expected that anyone would raise a hand, but did hope to appeal to their united sense of justice. She understood this neighborhood was a place where no one snitched from fear of being the next victim.

Taking a deep breath, she continued the next part of the eulogy, happy that Rob had the fore-sight to plan this surprise.

He was not fond of getting. His forte was in giving. He and Lenore had planned on gifting the community with something special that would please not only the citizens of Buffalo, but on a personal level, would cause Shelly immense joy.

*You who knew Father Rob, as a friend, as well as a priest, know that he had fought our plan to celebrate his tenure as a priest at this huge public structure. The only way we could get him to agree to all this hoopla was to have him approve the menu and his choice of music. Of course, we agreed. The result is what you are enjoying today, in his honor.*

*He also stated, emphatically, that this event was to be a fund-raiser for renovating the Terminal. Some of you may know that his generous trust-fund helped to pay for many people's climb out of poverty through education.*

Antoine and Marcus, were in the front row, and began clapping. In five seconds, others in the crowd joined in. They were the ones, also, helped by Rob's generosity. Jackson's fiancé was one of them, as were her sister, Mandy, and at least twenty others. The cameras began rolling. Jackson made sure to stay close to Lexie. He wanted all the positive exposure to feature him.

Merrill had witnessed her ex-husband's opportunistic actions, was sickened by them, and was thinking of telling her father she had to leave. She stayed because he father had asked her to look around the crowd, and try to notice anyone doing anything out of the ordinary. So far, everyone, except Jackson was behaving normally. He was behaving as if this was his personal photo op.

Lenore continued speaking:

*Rob was always thrilled when his efforts paid off. Not for his own glory, but because he truly believed that if one had the financial means, it was a God-given responsibility to share it with those in need. He lived the Eight Beatitudes and Works of Mercy, as much as followed the Ten Commandments.*

*Shelly, would you please join me up here, to reveal Father Rob's big surprise and hopefully, his lasting legacy?*

Tina was smiling as Shelly approached the podium. She was in on the plan, approved, and couldn't wait for the reveal.

Tia looked at her grandmother with questioning eyes. The three friends could barely conceal their happy glow. This was hardly the tear-jerking eulogy everyone had expected. It was Shelly's turn to take a deep breath and express what Rob had planned a month before this celebration.

*One evening, after enjoying one of our friend Tina's magnificent dinners, we sat on her deck over-looking Lake Erie, reminiscing, and wishing upon the brilliant stars. One of Rob's wishes was that he wanted to help out as many people as he could, with the inheritance his father had left him. It was an immense amount, and Rob couldn't imagine how he could spend it all during his life-time. He said, 'I know the trust-fund run by the Mission is doing a great job, but it's limited in space, and can just do so much.*

*I've been thinking about expanding my efforts by building a kind of inner-city boarding school, where more kids could be helped, and tutored, and given guidance. What do you girls think?'*

*He always called us his 'girls.' But that's not the only reason we adored him. Yes, he had charm, great looks, and was fun to be around, but he also possessed compassion, generosity, empathy, intelligence…every possible trait of a genuinely good person.*

*I'm the culprit of planting the seed for renovating this structure, the Central Terminal, for the purpose he had just wished for. I am devoted to preserving old buildings, as many of you generous donors know, from attending my fund-raisers.*

*Father Rob had helped many poor souls in need of all kinds of counseling: spiritual, financial, moral. He knew, better than most, that what he heard in the confessional could fill volumes of stories of people who were broken and needed fixing, or simply tune-ups. That's why he wished for a larger place than the Mission to fulfill the needs of so many Buffalo souls. He stated that wish aloud to us.*

*We were silent for a beat, then our heads, hearts, and minds began developing strategies and ideas at warp-speed. Rob wanted this to be a special place, and it already is. But we had to come up with the millions of dollars it would take to make his wish come true, and mine, in preserving this one of a kind structure.*

The crowd remained silent as residents from the Mission began distributing pamphlets. Each piece of literature featured a plan for what the Terminal could become and a pledge sheet. There was also a brief history of the building and the surrounding neighborhood, which was once the home of many Eastern European immigrants.

Shelly continued with what she and her friends had planned:

Merrill noticed that Jackson had folded the pamphlet and handed it to Lexie. She unfolded it, and read its contents, while her fiancé looked around, marking where influential rich people may be standing, so he could approach them after the eulogy. She thought he looked like a hunter, stalking his prey.

*This Central Terminal was designed by the same architects who are responsible for the New York Central Terminal. We realized that trains will not be needed for commuters in the near future, as high-speed tubular modes of transportation are already in the works.*

*To make a short story of our complex plans, Father Rob Sullivan has already donated 30 million dollars of his trust fund to this unique project in order to re-purpose this great building. He was going to ask for your support at this anniversary bash, as he liked to refer to it, instead of it being a mere celebration of his own life as a priest. This is already one million above what the current estimate is to renovate. He was going to ask people of substantial means, here today, to donate so that the boarding school would be in operation as a self-supporting entity, once the renovations are complete.*

*This was to be his way of using most of the money he had inherited, 'through no fault of my own,' he would laugh. His sense of humor was pure tonic for any world-weary soul, but he wanted something of substance to make more people joyful This is it.!*

Before Shelly could instruct how those wishing to donate could participate, a voice shouted out from the crowd. "I'll donate a million," followed by, "Make it two mill, from me."

*The News* cameras couldn't keep up with the verbal pledges. It seemed as if the donors wished to blend in with the crowd and remain anonymous. But cell phone cameras were clicking away like mad crickets.

The murmuring crowd couldn't subdue the voices of donors, pledging to support Father Rob's dream. The women smiled in sheer joy at the outpouring of generosity.

"I would like to make my donation in the amount of ten million," a voice boomed out from the edges of the crowd, near the front. Lenore, Shelly, and Tina, all turned in the direction of the voice to identify the generous donor. The crowded room was filled with gasps, but none larger than from the women's themselves. Standing on the edge of the crowd, in full view, was Father Rob Sullivan!

## Chapter 40

Of course, it was not the good priest offering such a generous donation. It was his doppelganger. Detective Foster immediately set the women straight when he saw their shocked faces. He told them the person who looked like Father Rob Sullivan was Dr. Justin Daniels, Jackson's father.

"But he looks more like Rob, than his own son," Lenore exclaimed.

"Let's all meet up at the Mission afterwards. There are things Rob didn't have time to explain to you."

"What kind of things?" Tina asked.

"New things he had just discovered about his own life, just a few days ago. Now, please excuse me. Your friend, Nicki seems to want my attention. She's been helping me scour the crowd for any leads in who may have a guilty conscience and look."

"Do you know what this new information is, Lenore?" Shelly thought they were aware of everything in each other's lives, past and present.

"No. But Martin said Rob had just learned of something new, about himself just a few days ago."

Harris came up to Lenore with a fistful of pledges, he and Leo had been collecting.

**"I am astonished, and extremely pleased by your outpouring of generosity,"** Lenore told the people in the terminal.

**"This is certainly the best possible way we could honor Father Rob Sullivan's life as a priest. I will send out an email, shortly, to everyone regarding the plans and progress we have made, for the renovation of this beautiful building to house, teach, and take care of those in need of us loving them as we love ourselves.**

**The Golden Rule is what Father Sullivan preached, and lived by. Now we can actually make his wish come true. Father Rob, I know you're here, listening, but mostly smiling."**

And as if on cue, the great clock in the concourse chimed, six times.

The crowd was deafeningly still for a minute, until cell phones began recording the sound of the clock speaking to them. *The News* teams went wild, trying to get statements from people. Lenore, Tina, and Shelly, made their escape from the podium just in time.

They shut themselves off from the gathering in a small room, that once was an office. Harris and Leo were there, organizing the pledges.

"Leo, thank you so much for helping out. Harris and I never thought there would be so many enthusiastic donors. A young woman was with him, also assisting.

Lenore remembered Rob had told her that Leo was engaged.

"I heard the good news from Rob, a few days ago, Leo. I'd like to offer congratulations."

"You must mean my promotion to work for C&V Fashions in New York."

"That too, but he told me you were planning on announcing your engagement to, I assume, this lovely lady at your side."

Leo looked confused. The young woman Lenore referred to turned bright scarlet.

"I'm so sorry. I may have spoken out of turn. Harris can confirm I do that sometimes."

Harris explained. "Lenore, this is Jennifer, Leo's assistant. She works for him."

"I haven't had time to make any romantic connections, yet," Leo smiled. "Carlos and Vanessa have kept me cutting patterns, designing, and now mentoring others in the business."

"I am so sorry, Jennifer. I'm Lenore, the person who helps run the Mission, with a foot in her mouth at times."

"No worries," Jennifer said. "Leo and I grew up together in the same neighborhood. He offered me a chance to better myself, paying forward like he was taught to do by your friends, Nicki and Father Rob."

"Every time I think there will be an end to the kindness chain, Rob began, I'm shown another link has been added." Lenore would have to try and recall what Rob had said about Leo, but now was not that time.

Tina and Shelly were closing down the food stations in the main concourse. The Memorial would be on *The News* and written about in the papers. More donations were sure to come in.

"I think Rob would be extremely pleased with the bash you and *his girls* created for him this afternoon, Lenore." Harris pulled his wife to him in a bear hug.

"I know he is, darling. It looks like we've collected enough pledges to, not only begin the renovation, but more than enough to keep it going for years to come."

"Leo and Jennifer were about to leave, when Lenore suddenly remembered the name Rob had used when referring to Leo's engagement.

"Do you know a young woman, named Melissa, Leo?"

"Can't think of anyone," Leo said.

"We went to school with a girl by that name, Leo. Remember how some of the kids teased her because of her name, calling her *Mill-asses*?"

"I was probably one of those teasers, I'm ashamed to say," Leo admitted.

"Well, no matter." Lenore said. "We elderly frequently mix up names."

But she was certain Rob had not been confused. She would try to find out if he had been mistaken, when she and the others were to meet with Martin at the Mission.


# Chapter 41


Harris had called ahead for pizza and wings to be delivered to the mission office. The women and he had not had time to partake of the food stations, Rob had requested to be set up featuring a menu of Buffalo favorites

Besides pizza and wings, there was roast beef, cannoli, pierogi, lasagna, and hot dogs. They were a huge success, as was the polka band that played more sedate classical Polish songs, rather than rousing dance music.

Everyone at the memorial service, was filled with peace, joy, and smiling. Not a tear was shed.

Everyone had something wonderful to say during the Memorial. They related personal stories of their connection with the priest. They loved that he was "everyman" and understood every woman.

Eating his favorite foods, they laughed that they had never attended such a happy, loving memorial service. They felt Father Rob's presence all around.

Several architectural firms and developers had left their cards along with their donations. Lenore would set up a Board of Directors to go through all the offers. This was going to be an enormous project.

It would also include a plan suggested to her by a University of Buffalo professor who offered a way to renovate the housing stock surrounding the Terminal. Lenore agreed with his concrete ideas of making City Hall move faster with getting vacant land-lords under control and initiating a way to give tax breaks to people who would buy and fix up the older homes in order to live in them, instead of flipping them. He had other great ways to make the neighborhood a viable part of the city.

The mayor had been a figure-head too long, and was confident he would be re-elected as long as he did the usual…nothing, while supporting the developers with big pockets.

Lenore was toying with a plan to get Jackson Daniels involved. He seemed to want a bigger political role. If he was willing to be a progressive politician, she would suggest he run for mayor. She would back him. It could be a win-win. First, she had to ask Martin about Jackson's relationship with his father and whether he was correct in assuming drugs were streaming in through the mission residents

"We did plan on announcing the renovation of the Terminal at the anniversary party," Lenore explained.

Tina, Shelly, Nicki, Harris were seated at the long conference table in the mission office, enjoying the food Harris had ordered, along with a few bottles of wine.

Martin Foster knocked politely, then entered the room.

"I see you all are more relaxed now, ready to carry out Rob's last wishes. I don't think he realized they would be his last, but, as he might say, *It is what it is.*"

"How long have you known Rob," Shelly asked. "You seem to have known him quite well, yet he never mentioned having you as a close friend."

"Right." Tina said. "He had us as his best friends. I don't think he had many male friends, except for you, of course, Harris."

"I can honestly admit, he and I became friends, within the last week. But, I've known him almost all my life."

"We're way too tired for riddles, Martin," Lenore complained. "You said you would share with us some new information about Rob that he had only learned about himself."

Martin nodded, sat down, then told the story of Judith Lee Silver's murder, his investigation, and its result. This was how he had come to introduce himself to the priest. He took a breath and dropped the bombshell. There was no easy way to say it, except bluntly.

"Rob learned that his parents were not his birth parents. He was adopted by them in re-payment of a debt owed to his father's business associate. The business associate was none other than Jason L. Daniels, Jackson's grandfather."

The listeners were in silent shock, trying to absorb this fact.

No one seemed capable of connecting the dots of the detective's statement. They could only stare and wait for more information.

"Rob was in shock, too, when he learned that his mother was the daughter of a family connected to an old mob family in Lewiston. I never could find out the name of his biological father. But, you've seen the person he is related to by birth. The man who looks exactly like Rob and who donated all those millions is Rob's uncle."

"What's his name?" Tina was able to ask first.

"Dr. Justin Daniels," Martin stated matter-of-factly.

"But…!" It began to dawn on Tina that this was the same last name as Jackson's.

"Correct assumption, Tina," Martin continued. "Dr. Justin Daniels is Jackson's father."

Nicki finally spoke. "That's why Jackson turned white as a sheet and quickly grabbed his fiancé to leave when he saw and heard his father donate the huge sum of money for the renovation."

"Rob looks… looked… more like a Daniels than Jackson does," Shelly noted.

"Unfortunately, there's more family drama there," Martin added.

"Dr. Daniels also began forming a close relationship with Rob, this past week. We found the three of us had much in common. We agreed to meet up every Thursday for a chat and refreshments, at the doctor's home-office on Delaware."

Martin did not go into what Justin had revealed about why he couldn't stand his step-son. He didn't even mention that Jackson was adopted. He did, however, reveal that Jackson was looking for a money source to fund his political ambitions. His father, Justin, had refused. This had made the two estranged. This was also why, as Nicki, had noted, he was so upset when his father donated such a large sum of money for the renovation, causing him to leave the terminal in a rage.

"Families can truly dole out the worst kind of poison to each other," Tina said. "Tia told me Jackson was a shallow person, capable of conning and cunning to get what he wanted. She dated him briefly, in college. Thank God she hadn't fallen for him."

"Sad to say, there are and were many women who fell hard. That's another reason why his own father feels sorry for Jackson's fiancé." Again, Martin did not go into the details of Jackson's liaisons with the fair sex and his father's repugnance of the way his son treated women..

"Do you think Rob would have told us all this, himself, Martin?" Nicki asked.

"Eventually. It was a bit much for him to absorb in such a short time. I'm sure he would have confided in you, after the party."

"We knew he was distracted by something," Lenore said. "But we were all too wrapped up in planning the party that we ignored his unusual silence."

"He had visited me at the vineyard to ask about a dream he had had," Nicki said. "I was waiting till after the party to ask him more about it. I won't reveal his dream, but now it makes sense that he must have found out what it meant. I can only say that it had to do with his family."

"I feel bad that we weren't there for him, the way he was always there for us," Shelly said,

"I hope I can allay your fears about that," Martin said. "He wasn't emotionally distraught. Mostly, he was amazed he had lived so long without ever knowing the truth. In fact, he was happy he never knew, otherwise he would never have inherited the vast amount of money his father had left him to do the most good with he could."

"I know he quickly tried to rid himself of that money, as if it burned him,' Lenore said. "The trust fund was his way of getting rid of it, in a worthwhile way."

"Lenore, you hold the Trust for him. Do you know, or can you tell us how much money Rob was left? I'm not being nosey," Shelly said. "It makes sense that we know how much money may be behind someone's intention in making his death look like a suicide."

Lenore looked around the room at the people she trusted most in life, and the ones Rob had trusted as well.

Martin agreed. "Usually when there's this kind of homicide, there's a money trail to follow. It certainly wasn't a power play. Rob wasn't involved with the Vatican or even Diocesan politics. If there is a large amount of money involved, even in a trust fund, there's bound to be someone who wants control of it."

"Hold on to your hats, then." Lenore said. "Rob was left at least 50 million by his father's estate, and it keeps growing quarterly."

No one said a word, until Martin finally confirmed what they were all beginning to think.

"There must be someone who wanted in on that much money. I think if we discover the person who had the most to gain…we'll discover the person or persons responsible for Rob not being here to attend his own party."

"Except, I truly believe and sense, he is here, waiting for us to figure it all out," Nicki said confidently.

"I agree," Tina admitted.

"Me, too," said Shelly.

"Me three," Lenore chimed in.

"And I'll have to fourth that," Harris said. "If his spirit wasn't still here to hold you all up, you'd all be helpless messes, unable to function as well as you have been."

"If anything, we seem to stronger than ever," Nicki said. "I told Lowell I wouldn't be returning to Canada, until all this is solved."

"Then we'd better get to work," Lenore said. "Tell us where and how to start, Martin."


## Chapter 42


Martin was able to coordinate the efforts of the women in finding out who may have been implicated in Rob's demise. He informed them that because the pills were left in Rob's desk, they could rule out anyone who would sell them for a profit.

"The street value of the 200 pills is well over $6,000.00. That much money would eliminate the residents of the mission, or the street gangs as suspects."

"But what if someone paid them off even more to plant the pills there?"

"That's very true, Lenore. Harris has never been one to trust as much as you. He's already set in place informants throughout the mission to warn him of any potential illegal problems. They're net-working as we speak, to see if anyone has come into unexplained riches."

"Who's going to snitch on the gangs. No one says a peep even if one of their own is killed. They're too afraid of retaliation."

"This is also true, Shelly. The police task force on gang activity has not seen any evidence of collusion by their plants that would make them suspect a gang banger of this type of plan. The gangs shoot, kill, then run. They don't stage."

"Do you think it was done by someone Rob knew?" Shelly asked. I've been wracking my brain, but come up empty."

"We agree that this was pre-meditated," Tina said. "I've asked Tia to look into Jackson and his father's family dynamics. She has a good friend who knows Jackson's fiancé and his secretary as well. They went to school together, back in the day, and lived in the same trailer park with them."

"Was she one of Rob's human success stories?" Lenore asked.

"Tia told me her friend went to Canisius on Father Rob's dime. She's a successful attorney now, but still hangs with her friends from before, who also made it up the ladder out of poverty and failure.

Lexie is Jackson's fiancé, but she's also his father, Dr. Daniels' nurse. Tia's friend, Mara, is even going to be one of Lexie's bridesmaids. Mandy, Lexie's sister is Jackson's secretary. Tia told me there's a problem already, in that Mandy refuses to stand up for Lexie's marriage to Jackson. There's going to be twelve bridesmaids in all.""

"Tina's grand-daughter is correct." Martin said. "I won't go into the details, but there's a reason between Mandy not wanting to be bridesmaid and Lexie's confusion as to that reason. Dr. Daniels already explained the reason to me and Father Rob, but it has nothing to do with this case, so we won't pursue that avenue of possible leads. See if Tia can find out more about Jackson from Mara, Tina. It would be helpful to know how he came to be acquainted with these women from such different backgrounds as his own."

"Forgive my next question, Martin, but your own daughter was married to Jackson. Surely she knows more about him than anyone else." Lenore felt embarrassed having to bring up Martin's daughter, Merrill.

"It isn't relevant, either, Lenore. I wish it was. But, my daughter can't explain his relationship with these women, either. After they were divorced, she had nothing to do with him, and they didn't travel in the same circles. Jackson even gave up parental rights to his own sons. He did try to seek alimony from my daughter, as she was left a large trust fund by my late wife's estate. I knew about this, because we had discussed it, before my wife succumbed to cancer. We both felt our daughter had made a huge mistake and would need some means of support after we were gone. I didn't need or want anything besides my pension.

When Jackson found out he was to get nothing, he spitefully severed all ties to my daughter and their children. Luckily, the boys were too young to understand their father's actions. Dr. Daniels began acting as a surrogate father, as have I."

"That little story has changed my mind about approaching Jackson for a possible run for mayor, that I was going to back. His baggage is way too heavy. No wonder he's seeking a seat in Albany, where such scandals are buried."

"My brother-in-law, John, is a State Senator," Shelly said. "But his scandalous past is nothing compared to Jackson's."

"Can anyone think of a reason for Jackson to want Rob out of his way?" Martin asked. "No one is off the table as a suspect. That includes myself...as well as you ladies."

"What?!!! Are you really suggesting that one of us had anything to do with this?" Tina asked angrily.

"I'm only suggesting that you be aware that I will turn over everyone's past in order to find motive. If you have nothing to hide, there'll be no subpoenas from me. But, if you need to confess. This is the right time and place."

"Don't be too upset, girls," Lenore coaxed. "Martin's right. Many crimes have been committed by those closest to the victim."

"Fine. But whatever you may be looking for, won't be in my private domain, unless someone's planted it there." Tina valued her privacy, and that included resenting anyone going through her volumes of diaries, she kept up with since she received one as a birthday present when she was 12.

"So, what do you suggest we do to help find the culprit?" asked Shelly.

"For now, carry on business as usual. Lenore has the names of people who are competing with each other for the renovation job of the Central Terminal. Lenore and Harris will take note of any bid that seems sketchy or way off."

"Tina, you keep in contact with Tia and inform me immediately of any, even tiny bit of information that she may have from her friend, Mara. It could be the piece that makes the entire puzzle, whole."

"Shelly, you try and find out what connection the girls Jackson has working for him have with each other. We know Lexie and Mandy are sisters. We know they went to school with a girl named, Mara. There are too many women surrounding Jackson, who are from such different backgrounds. I'd like to see what they all have in common."

"So do I," announced Lenore. "Tomorrow I'll be paying a visit to City Hall, not only to meet with Jackson, but to also scope out his secretary Mandy, and ask her how she feels about her sister's up-coming marriage to Jackson."

"Let's all meet back here on Friday to compare notes," Martin instructed. "I'm not wasting time trying to figure this out by myself. This is a case where the more leads we follow, the more we can come to the end of this journey."

"Sadly, this is a road I wish we never had to go down," Shelly said.

Everyone bowed their heads in silent agreement.

Once again, the silence was broken by the tolling of the bell in the church's tower across the courtyard.

"That's strange," Harris stated. "That bell hasn't been tolled in years. I'm not sure it's still even in working order."

Nicki smiled. "I guess that's Rob's way of making sure we heard him. He's still with us, and won't be leaving till we're good and ready to let him go."

"If that's true, Rob; I'll be baking some pies this week, just for you. Somehow, you'll let me know what I should do with them, since I know you won't be able to enjoy them now." Tina was sure Rob wouldn't let her down. He never had.

## Chapter 43

Lenore had a plan. She wasn't about to wait for the police or anyone else to stand in her way when she knew how to force the truth out of people sooner rather than later. She had learned much about dealing with all kinds of people in her career as an interior decorator, and as someone running a mission where she had to determine who was an honest person in need of assistance or who was simply looking for easy hand-outs.

She had discussed her plan with her husband, who agreed it was a good one. He also gave her more hints as to how to get people to "fess" up. Previously, he had been part of the anti-terror force, and was used to getting information from people without them even knowing what he was doing to pry open their secrets.

"Be subtle, Lenore," he advised. "Don't be direct. Plant discord in their mind-set. Confuse them as to the facts. Make them feel insecure. Make them feel you are on their side and can be trusted to protect them. Gain their confidence. In most cases, the people who know the truth are anxious to be relieved of it. Be their confessor."

Armed with her experience and Harris's advice, Lenore walked into Jackson's office, confidently, smiling graciously at Mandy, Jackson's secretary. She would be the first line of defense to disarm.

"Hi Mandy. Leo introduced us at Father Rob's Memorial. It's always such a pleasure to meet people Rob has touched with his generosity. He was able to help you and your sister, Lexie, I believe, when both of you were in need. I also met someone named Mara, who was part of that group Father Rob helped. Leo's so proud of all he's been able to accomplish. I'm sure you, your sister, and others like Mara are also proud of their present circumstances. I also hear congratulations are in order for your sister's up-coming marriage to your boss, Jackson Daniels."

The look on Mandy's face told Lenore, she had managed to confuse the poor young woman as well as upset her. She wanted to give her plenty to think about while she met with Jackson. Before Mandy could respond, Jackson opened his office door.

"Lenore, it's always a pleasure to meet with you. Even amidst these unpleasant circumstances. Condolences, once more for your dear friend's death. Mandy, please hold all my calls till Lenore and I are finished with our meeting."

Lenore had to admit Jackson was not only handsome, but charming, as well as sophisticated in his manner. He would have made a wonderful mayor, if appearances were the only qualification. The hint of a political office was the hook she needed to gain an appointment with him at such short notice. She told Mandy that she wished to speak to Jackson about the possibility of backing him as a mayoral candidate.

Jackson had coffee and Danish laid out in a show of hospitality.

"I really was impressed at the Memorial. You refrained from behaving like the shallow politician many are, in using the opportunity to schmooze to gain public and private backing. That ability to behave like a normal human being gave me pause to consider you as a possible mayoral candidate whom I would like to endorse and back, financially. As you know, I, as well as my husband, and friends are extremely dedicated to making Buffalo the Queen City again. We need good leaders to continue our progressive momentum."

Jackson couldn't dim the glow spreading across his face. There was no need to ask if he was interested in her proposition, but she asked anyway.

She didn't want to confuse Jackson the way she had Mandy. She wanted him to be perfectly clear about her offer to finance his campaign, if he agreed to run for mayor.

She had baited the trap and was waiting for him to take it. He certainly did.

Now, all she had to do was see how things played out.

"Lenore, I'm honored, to say the least, by this offer. I've always had this city's well-being as my main concern. That's why I was contemplating moving to Albany as a Buffalo constituent. I felt that is where I could exert some influence. But, as its mayor, I believe I could have much more influence in convincing our Albany seats of power that Buffalo is deserving of far more than what we are presently doled out."

"I agree, Jackson. Our current mayor is really a ribbon-cutting figure-head, taking credit for the progress others have achieved. I think the right person in charge of the city could really go on to even being a governor."

Jackson almost jumped from his chair in joy. He was more enthusiastic about Lenore's proposal than she had expected.

"There is one tiny reservation I have, Jackson, before I get you too committed to my idea. I noticed your ex-wife at the Memorial. When she entered with Detective Foster, I thought she was his companion. I learned she's his daughter. Then, a friend of mine told me as your ex-wife, there is an acrimonious relationship. I hope this won't be a problem in my backing you. I know you're planning on re-marrying. But, I also hope your divorce from Merrill, could be determined to be amicable, at least by the public."

Jackson was quiet, trying to find the right words to assure Lenore that he would be an honorable candidate with no scandalous baggage.

"Can I get your assurance that your past marriage won't bring up fires I'll be having to put out?"

Jackson nodded, putting on his most serious face.

"I guarantee there will be no problems. I can take care of anything that may come up, although there won't be anything."

Jackson decided to try the high road and explained, "The divorce was not pleasant. No divorce is. But, I tried to make the marriage work. Merrill resisted and was greatly influenced by her parents who disliked me. They thought I was beneath her because I had no family estate or money. Merrill's father had no money of his own either. He's a detective, for God's sake. But for some reason, they thought I was unworthy of their daughter.

My own father is a highly-respected doctor. He isn't one to squander or parade his wealth in public. I must admit, when he made such a generous donation for the renovation of the Central Terminal, I was shocked, indeed. He is usually very frugal. I didn't even know he possessed such an enormous amount of money to be able to donate, so freely."

Lenore could see this new fact still bothered him.

"I take it he didn't spoil you, while you were growing up? He must have taught you that ethics and morals were more important than a huge pile of cash."

This statement seemed to confuse Jackson for a minute. He rebounded. "Of course. My father was a strict disciplinarian who made me work for everything in order to teach me the value of things, but especially the value of people."

"Do you think Merrill would be able to support your bid for mayor's office?"

Again, Jackson hesitated, but replied, "She may try to slander me because of the divorce, but I may be able to convince her that the past is gone, and it's time to reconcile our differences for the good of the children, and this city."

"You have children?"

"Yes. Two boys, I've been unable to help raise because of the family's disinheritance of me. They have the money, so they have the power to erase me from my own children's lives."

Lenore was amazed at how smoothly Jackson could twist the truth to suit his own version of it. She almost gave away her opinion of this lie with a smirk, but was able to control herself and smiled sweetly.

"Then, perhaps we can meet next week to further discuss my proposition. In the meantime, you might be able to clear up anything that might hinder your ability to present yourself to the public as the up-standing citizen, I'm sure you are. It wouldn't hurt to get other influential people to rate your suitability. Family members can be helpful, but are really too biased to convince others of positive traits."

Jackson's wheels were turning at warp speed, but he was able to thank Lenore for her confidence in him and assure her that he was the person she could count on to make Buffalo the Queen city it once was.

On her way out, Lenore noticed that Mandy had a slight frown on her face. She was pleasant to Lenore, though, and managed to smile.

"Hope to see you soon, Mandy. Jackson will explain our wonderful productive meeting to you, I'm sure."

She was about to leave, when another young woman with large earrings and one of Leo's signature designer outfits entered the office.

"Hi Mandy, is the boss in?"

Mandy's frown deepened as the young woman ignored Lenore and proceeded to knock on Jackson's door, letting herself in with out hesitation.

"A pushy kind of person, that one?" Lenore was referring to the young woman who had rushed passed her.

Mandy replied, "That one is Melissa. Another old friend from the neighborhood. Jackson got her a job here in City Hall. You'd think she owned the place. Thinks she'll be the next mayor of Buffalo."

"She's not the only one," Lenore laughed, heading for the elevators.

A few minutes later, she realized why that young woman's name was familiar. It was the name Rob had given her as being Leo's fiancé. The woman who had called to set up an appointment to discuss marriage plans.

This was something worth discussing with Martin and the others. Her visit to City Hall was going to unravel some puzzles, as well as some people…like Mandy.

# Chapter 44

When Melissa left Jackson's office, Mandy was asked to enter and bring her address and phone book. Jackson needed her to come up with his ex-wife's phone number. It was time to reverse gears for him.

"Why are you calling Merrill?"

"You know…I want to tell her I'm getting re-married and to let bygones be bygones. I want to have a relationship with our sons."

"But I thought you dis-owned them?"

"I was acting out of anger, Mandy. We all do selfish stupid things when we're enraged. Do you recall how old they are now?"

"They're 7 and 8." She replied testily. "Do you even remember their names?"

"What crawled up your butt? Isn't it about time I started taking an interest in my own sons?"

Lenore's plan of getting Mandy upset had taken root.

"And what was that skank, Melissa doing here?"

"That's no way to talk about one of your best friends, Mandy."

"Stop it, Jackson! You know she's best friends with Lexie. That's why you got her a job here. I don't like how she waltzes in here whenever she wants and takes advantage of you."

"I like her, Mandy. And so does your sister. She's even going to be a bridesmaid. Why won' t you be one too? Lexie loves you and you're her only sister."

"You wouldn't understand," Mandy said, slamming Jackson's door behind her.

She was upset, knowing that Jackson didn't even know she had once carried his child. She was relieved now, knowing what a hypocrite he could be that she had mis-carried. She knew his father, Dr. Daniels, who she had confided in when she was pregnant, was a much better human being than his son. She also knew the doctor understood, better than anybody what Jackson was really like.

Her thoughts were interrupted by Jackson's appearance in front of her desk.

"Mandy, call all your friends: Leo, Mara, and others you grew up with, and yes, Melissa too. I'm taking Lexie and all of you out to dinner as a better-late- than- never engagement party. I've been so busy, I need to make it up to Lexie and show her how much our up-coming marriage means to me by celebrating with her friends, soon to be my own. See if everyone can make it this Friday. And make the reservation for us all at Russell's."

When Jackson returned to his own desk, Mandy almost slammed out of the office. She was absolutely beside herself with rage. But, of course, she didn't flee. She got out her address book and dutifully did what Jackson had requested.

Everyone had responded that they would be delighted to accept the invite to dinner. Mandy did note some less than happy tone in Melissa's voice when she learned it was to celebrate Lexie and Jackson's engagement.

"Lexie doesn't realize how lucky she is to be marrying Jackson," she had sighed to Mandy.

That's when Mandy realized Mellissa was enamored with Jackson, the same way she had been once. She decided she had to make one more call before leaving for the day.

"Lexie? Does Dr. Daniels have an opening today? I have a scratchy throat, and want to nip it in the bud. You know I'm susceptible to strep."

"Of course, Mandy. Come right over. I'll fit you in. You are my sister, after all."

Mandy was grateful she didn't harangue her again about not standing up for her wedding.

"I won't be here to welcome you. I have a gown fitting. Dr. Daniels will come out to greet you. I'll tell him to expect you."

"Thanks. And Lexie? Thanks for not laying into me about your wedding. I've had a rough day."

"Anything I can do?"

"No. It's probably the infection in my throat taking its toll."

"Is Jackson still there?"

"Yes."

"Connect us, please, will you? I want to get is approval on hiring a band I heard for our reception."

"Where were they playing?"

"At this concert I went to with Melissa. They played during lunch time in Lafayette Square."

"Wouldn't that be too much for a wedding? I mean the music?"

"No. They're soft rock and 80's love songs."

"That sounds great, then."

Mandy wasn't angry in the least with her sister. She knew that Jackson's true colors would be shown to her soon enough. Mandy had made up her mind to be there for her sister when that time came and it would. That's why she needed to talk with Dr. Daniels. She needed him to say that it was fine to support her sister's choice to marry Jackson, even if she didn't approve of that decision, herself. Her love for her sister could over-come her hate for Jackson.

# Chapter 45

Jackson waited for Mandy to leave, before he called Merrill. It would be a difficult call to make but an absolutely necessary one, if he ever hoped to become Buffalo's new mayor.

There was a chance she wouldn't even speak with him. He made sure he had a stiff drink for courage and to make his words sound soft and sweet. He knew all of Merrill's weak spots. He prided himself for knowing more about manipulating women than anyone he had ever known.

His acquaintances begged for the secret to his success with the ladies. He had no real male friends. His only advice to them was, "Make them believe you are their best friend. You are the only one they can trust. The rest will follow." It always had for him.

He was ecstatic when Merrill agreed to meet him for dinner. He didn't object when she suggested a newer restaurant downtown, named for the Area Code, *716*. She said that a public place was better than some place out of the way for obvious reasons, being they weren't trying to hide anything from anyone. He was also happy that she was so easy in her demeanor.

The last time they had spoken was at one of their numerous court dates, concerning the children, after their divorce, which must have been at least five years ago. She was more frigid to him than the ice queen she had become after discovering one of his numerous extra-marital affairs. It wasn't as if his on-the side liaisons had caused her any embarrassment. She could have had something on the side, too, if she had wanted to. Open marriages were healthy.

Their divorce had made the papers, as Merrill was left a huge trust fund from her parents, who were part of Buffalo's elite society. It infuriated him that he was left with nothing. Ever since the public humiliation he had suffered because of the big stink she had made, he avoided the social scene, determined to make his fortune by other means. So far, nothing lucrative had panned out.

The best way for him to make his way to the top was through politics. He had the necessary physical attributes. He looked handsome enough; Could schmooze with the best; and could make speeches without promising anything. He had become the city's Comptroller by going to night school at a community college, earning an Associate's Degree in Accounting, but most importantly, making connections with local politicians behind the scenes, and drumming up substantial contributions from people he knew had money because of his marriage to Merrill.

When he discovered his father was doling out pain pills to his patients, and charging them a mere $20.00 per office visit, his wheels started turning. He didn't know how to capitalize on this, until recently. His father would never give up his source of the pills, but there were other ways to make use of this information. He knew that turning his father into the authorities was counter-productive, as that would end the pill flow. Lenore had opened up an entire web of opportunity for him. He would organize the transformation of himself as an opportunist into a caring philanthropist, who would also run Buffalo as its mayor, and receive all the perks that were attached to public office.

Everything was falling into place, nicely. He wondered why Merrill had insisted on "716", in the heart of Canalside, but didn't want her to think he was still the same old bossy Jackson. He was willing to twist himself into Prince Charming, if it would claim her needed endorsement to be successful as a politician.

He could stop fuming over how his original plan of how to attain wealth had gone bad.. Right now, he was going to pursue this path to success. He would be a fool not to.

Lenore had generously laid it out for him. Enough of groveling before his father. There couldn't be much more left in his estate, anyway, after the generous donation he had made at Sullivan's Memorial. The priest was worth more, dead than alive.

He was going to put away his thoughts about how the original plan had failed. This new path proved to be perfect. If only it had come before Melissa and her old friend had botched everything up. No matter. Nothing could be traced to him. If anything, Melissa's old loser friend would take the blame. Druggies always lost. Thank God, he refused to be tempted into selling those pills. Easy money, or not.

He didn't tell Mandy about his dinner plans with Merrill. He made the reservations himself. The less the girls from Lexie's circle of family and friends knew, the better. He would announce his plans at the dinner he was hosting for them at Russell's. Nothing like disarming people by taking them to an expensive, restaurant, and up the carte blanche check.

Mandy entered his office, confirming she had made reservations for the exclusive dinner.

"Why did you invite Melissa?" She asked with an edge.

"She's part of the old group, isn't she? The people you and Lexie grew up with?"

"But she's not part of our group now. Somehow, she found a way to become Lexie's friend. She's pushy and her motive for being so nice to you is her own advancement."

"Isn't that what successful people do? They push their way in, until doors start to open, freely?"

"I went to college for my advancement. So did Lexie. Leo's got talent and earned a spot at the Fashion Institute. Mara's also full of talent. That's why Leo's mentoring her and Jennifer."

"And what would you say Melissa's talent is, Mandy?"

"I could be vulgar, but I'll only say she's able to get what she wants by using her looks, sex, and outlandish boldness."

"She is very pretty, don't you think? Her hair falls in those soft ringlets around her face. Those huge blue eyes and cupid bow's mouth? Do you think she has a big mouth?"

"Now you're being vulgar, Jackson, and it's making me sick."

"No. No. Take your smart mind out of the gutter. I meant does she blab or gossip a lot?"

"I think she'd do or say anything to get what she wanted."

"You're being awfully nasty today, Mandy, dear. What put that bee in your bonnet? Do you have a new boyfriend who upset you?"

Mandy did not hear his last question. She had already slammed out of his office.

# Chapter 46

Martin made sure Lexie had left for the day when he went to meet Justin and his daughter Merrill, two hours before Jackson was to take Merrill to dinner.

"What if I can't pull it off," Merrill asked. "I mean it sickened me to see him at the Memorial, and to be sitting across a dinner table with him could lead to one of two things. I could throw up, or start screaming at him for being such a shitty father to the boys."

"Would you rather have him in your life, or out, Merrill? Aren't the boys better off knowing as little of their father until they're old enough to make their own judgment about him?"

"I know, Dad. But, Jesus, what if he really did change? What then? Should I ask him back into our lives?"

She hadn't really spoken to Jackson for almost five years! What if she found herself falling for him all over again? He still had charm…was still very handsome, and Merrill hadn't dated anyone since the divorce. Could she trust herself to be strong? She was going up against a master con artist.

"Whoa, there little lady," Justin demanded. "I'm Jackson's father. I assure you, he hasn't changed; wouldn't know how to begin to, or why. He likes himself too much. His selfishness is in-born. I don't know how or why. His mother was a wonderful person. But take my word for it, please. Jackson is still a narcissistic sociopath. Only intense therapy and behavior modification can change someone like that. And he's receiving no treatment whatsoever, because he likes what he is."

"Why is he able to con so many women into falling for him?"

Both her father and the doctor stared, in silence.

"I know. I fell for him, because I was naïve, and swept off my feet. But can't your nurse, Lexie, see him for who he really is? Haven't you warned her?"

"You know no one's heart can be talked out of a fatal situation. It's like getting a heart attack. It can hit without warning, or can be fatal if the warning signs are ignored."

"Spoken like a true doctor," Martin said. "But that's why we asked you to have this dinner with him, Merrill. We've explained our plan."

"If it works, it's a good one, I admit," Merrill said stoically. "If I can save one woman from his evil clutches, it's worth a few hours of disgust. But, you also said something about Lexie and pills."

"Right now, know that we're only attempting to find out if the pills Lexie was taking from Justin's stock and supplying them to someone else were the ones planted on Father Rob's desk, or if they were sold on the street. Jackson doesn't have the kind of money to run a successful campaign. We need to find out if there is a connection between him and the pills. We already know the person in the middle getting the pills from Lexie."

"Will Lexie get into legal trouble?"

"No, Merrill," Justin explained. "I've arranged for that to never happen. But don't worry about that now. Please try to enjoy dinner, and the show Jackson will put on for you. Be entertained, but not swayed by his charming persona. It's a fake. It's a way for him to get what he wants. It's never failed him in the past. It may be time for it to bite him back, hard, now."

"Do you want me to call you when I'm done?"

"That would be appreciated, Merrill. The good doctor will be asleep, but you know I hardly ever go to bed until the wee hours of the morn. I'll be waiting to hear from you."

Merrill turned to leave, but not before her father built up her confidence even more.

"And my darling daughter, you look gorgeous, absolutely ravishing. If your great beauty, charm, and intelligence, couldn't make Jackson willing to change, nothing on this earth can"

The two men sat silently for a while, sipping their brandy, hoping for the best.

"Do you think poor Lexie will survive this, Justin?"

"Oh, I don't doubt her heart will be broken. Her tears will be endless. But better a few months in purgatory than a life-time in hell."

"I can see you and Rob had much in common, Justin. You both have glib tongues and flowery language skills."

"I could blame it on Rob's Irish heritage, Marty. But then, there's more British in us than Irish."

"Well then, point proven. Wasn't Shakespeare English?"

"Looks like your nose for facts hasn't dulled a bit, Detective. Cheers!"

# Chapter 47

"If you're not feeling well, Lexie, you certainly should call it a day and go home?"

Justin felt bad that the medicine he and Marty had concocted to save Lexie from the Jackson syndrome was harsh, but obviously was proving effective.

"I'm physically fine, Dr. Daniels, but I'm miserable beyond anything I've ever felt." Lexie burst into sobs.

"Oh, my dear girl," Justin was truly sympathetic, handing his nurse a tissue, and allowing her to continue sobbing within his fatherly arms. "Is someone you love, sick? Did someone die? Is it your sister?"

"Nothing like that, Doctor. My heart is broken, and I don't know what to do?"

"Can I help?"

"May I tell you what happened? Maybe you can give me some advice. It does have to do with your son."

"He's hurt you? Tell me. Maybe I can help."


"My sister, Mandy, was at my door this morning with the early edition of the *News* in her hand, opened to the society page. There, plastered in living color was a photo of Jackson, toasting his ex-wife Merrill at *716!* I can't believe it! He told me he severed ties with the entire family, years ago, after the divorce. He doesn't even see his own kids."

Justin let her sobbing subside before he asked her if she knew why he wasn't seeing his children.

"He told me Merrill and her family prevented it. They hate him so much they made up some story about him being an abusive father, and the courts believed it. He also wasn't able to pay child support, so they used that as an excuse for non-parental rights as well."

"Do you know that I frequently visit with Merrill and my grandchildren?"

"No," Lexie said softly.

"I do, and there is nothing stopping Jackson from doing the same."

"But the courts ordered him to stay away from all of them!"

"Lexie, I'm sorry, but Jackson wasn't being truthful with you. He isn't seeing them because he thinks this is a way to punish Merrill and her family for throwing him out on his keister. He's made it a public lie that he was the one unfairly treated in the divorce. He's made Merrill and her family the villains."

"I don't believe that, Dr. Daniels. I'm surprised you do."

"What do you believe, Lexie?"

"I think Jackson's wife wants to get back with him. She made it clear by the way she's gazing at him in the photo with puppy dog eyes. And the headline screams, '*New Day for A Loving Couple.*'

The article goes onto quote, '*Merrill Foster wants her hubby back. The children are looking forward to having their Daddy back, too.*' The reporter said, '*The couple divorced in haste over family feuding, but were still really in love.*''

It ends with '*True love conquers all...even family squabbles like Shakespeare's Romeo and Juliet.*' The writer called it *a modern-day tragedy, made right*. What should I do, Doctor?"

"Have you spoken with Jackson about this?"

"He won't answer my texts or his cell. I think he's trying to break up with me, I honestly do." Lexie burst into sobs, again.

"What did your sister say about this?"

"Mandy? She tried to comfort me by saying he's a lying cheat. Can you imagine how that must have felt? I asked her to leave, and kept trying to call Jackson. I even went to his apartment?"

"And?"

"He wasn't there. The doorman said he hadn't checked in at all that evening and probably slept at his office. I couldn't go there, because the building doesn't open till 10:00 AM."

"Do you want me to call him?"

"Could you?…please? I need to make sure he's at least, safe. See if he'll tell you what's really going on."

"Come sit down. I've made a pot of tea. Try sipping some, while I make the call."

Lexie obeyed the doctor's orders. She felt calmer, knowing someone older and wiser than she was going to straighten this whole thing out.

"Do you mind if I put him on speaker mode?"

The young woman nodded her consent, putting on a brave face. Hearing Jackson confirm his innocence would make everything bad go away.

*"Dad, Hi. I was just about to call you. I was afraid you'd be with patients already, but I'm so glad we can talk. I've got some wonderful news. You'll be happy to learn you may be speaking with the next mayor of Buffalo."*

Justin feigned surprise. He was enjoying his role in this charade.

"Are you serious? What's happened to make this a possibility?"

This was becoming way too easy, because Justin knew his step-son's heart, inside and out. It was non-existent.

He knew his life would have turned out much differently if Charlie was still alive. He also knew living n the past was a waste, especially when his days were so limited in number now.

*"Lenore Burns from the Mission, approached me yesterday, telling me she was impressed with my work in City Hall, and wanted to know if I was interested in running for mayor. She was looking for a progressive candidate and would fully back my run, if I was interested."*

"I'm assuming you are?"

*"Dad, I'm more excited about this than anything else."*

"I saw your photo in the morning papers with Merrill. Is there a connection here?"

*"Thank God, Merrill's on board. She wants to get back together again for the sake of our children. She even admitted that being the mayor's wife would be a real feather in her society hat. Can you believe it?"*

"But what about Lexie? Aren't you planning on marrying her?" Justin glanced at Lexie, sitting with her head down, looking defeated, but no longer sobbing, with the wet tissue clenched in knuckle-white hands.

*"Lexie's young. She'll understand, once she gets over it. It's not right for a father not be able to raise his own children. Besides, once I'm elected, she and I can still have a relationship. Discreet, of course."*

Justin handed the receiver to Lexie, gesturing whether she wanted to comment. She simply shook her head. He turned off the speaker.

"Let me know how I can help, Jackson. I know Lenore has many powerful friends and lots of money to throw at a campaign. But if you need me to talk with Merrill more about this, you know I never stopped seeing her or the children."

*"You could help me out, Dad, with Lexie. Try to explain to her how this is my chance to make it. I know she wants me to be happy, I could never be happy with her if I knew she made a fuss about all this. Talk to her, Dad. Please. I know she loves you like her own father. She trusts you. Could you handle this for me, Dad?"*

"I can try," Justin said, not surprised to see the seat Mandy had been sitting in, now empty.

## Chapter 48

"I can't believe I'm such a damn fool." Lexie had left Justin's office after hearing the exact words of betrayal from her fiance's lips. She kept turning her engagement ring around her finger, trying to decide whether to keep it or throw it in his face.

"What can you say to me, Mandy, that'll make me feel less hurt and more anger?"

Mandy couldn't tell her that she had tried to warn her. She also wasn't about to confess that she had once carried Jackson's baby, and miscarried, while he an Merrill were still married.

"There's nothing I can say, right now, Lex, that'll make that kind pain disappear. Your heart and your pride were hurt. Right now is not the time to make some hasty decisions. Let's think on in it for a few, then decide what we should do."

"We?"

Mandy felt this was the time she could really stand up for her sister. Being her Maid of Honor would have been a farce.

"Did you think I'd let my baby sister fight this all alone? Jackson needs to be a taught a lesson no one ever bothered to teach him before. He's never had to face any consequences for his actions. Maybe if he had, this whole mess would never have happened."

"I knew him wanting to marry me was too good to be true. We're from the wrong side of the tracks, Mandy. We've come far, but we'll never be able to erase where we come from."

Mandy looked at her in horror. "Don't you ever, I mean never, think that way again. Just because we're not well off, doesn't mean we don't have morals or ethics…things that count. We're richer in those important things. Jackson is a pauper where real value is concerned."

Mandy's lecture brought a tiny smile to her sister's face.

"See you're beginning to heal over, already. You've been scarred by love, Lexie. That's a badge of honor."

"Don't be so dramatic, Mandy. Stop already."
They both burst out laughing, which was interrupted by Mandy's cell.

"Shit. It's him. He probably wants to know why I'm not in the office kissing his ass."

Lexie raised her eyebrows in surprise. She thought her sister adored her boss and her job.

"Hi, Jackson. Yes, I know I never called in. You want me to cancel the reservations I made at Russell's? There's been a change of plans? Have I spoken with my sister? Yes. She's upset. You want me to talk to her? Sure. I'll have plenty of time to console her because Jackson, darling…I quit!"

She closed her cell, cutting her boss off, and Mandy's smile was wide and serene.

"I should be telling you not to quit, Mandy. But really? This is the best news I've heard in quite a few hours. Thanks."

"I should have done this years ago, when he made me lie and cover for him with Merrill. She's not the bad person here. Jackson wanted everyone to believe he was her victim. I know he cheated on her, lied, and even gave up his own kids as a way to avoid paying child support."

"I know I wouldn't listen to you if you had told me all this before. Is this the reason you didn't want to be my Maid of Honor?" Lexie asked softly.

"Mostly. I couldn't see myself in that role. Somehow the word *honor* and Jackson don't mesh."

"Now I have to call my other bridesmaids and tell them the bad news."

"Look at it as good news. But, don't you have to tell the prospective bridegroom first?"

"I can't, Mandy. I don't ever want to see his face."

"Why not do it the easy way? Text him… then ghost him."

"You're right, He doesn't deserve a civilized courteous acknowledgment of our broken engagement."

Lexie used Mandy's phone in case Jackson had already ghosted her.

*This is your ex-fiance, Lexie. Fuck you, Jack-ass. And I'm keeping the ring…not to sell…but as an award for finally learning a lesson for life. Hope you lose, loser.*

"Wow! Looks like the crying part is over."

"For now," Lexie admitted. "I know I'll still feel bad, but you've come through as the best sister in the world."

"Now let me help you start cancelling all the wedding stuff. And with all the money you'll be saving, we're going on our own honeymoon. Any place you think you'd like to visit?"

"Let's rent an RV and tour the West!"

"Sounds good, *pardner*. Maybe we'll round us up some cowboys."

Mandy was thrilled her sister was spared being annihilated by Jackson. It surprised her how easy it finally was to free herself from him, as well. She didn't know where all her courage and smarts had come from, but she knew she would never find herself in a no-win situation like that again. She was certain Lexie had also learned that money and looks are meaningless when possessed by a devil. Neither one of them would ever be fooled again.

"I already know who will be my replacement as Jackson's secretary," Mandy predicted.

"You do?

"One of your bridesmaids."

"Who? I did ask twelve, you know."

"The one we grew up with who wants to be the next Mrs. Daniels, since you broke up with him."

"I'm in no mood, Mandy...Who?

"Melissa. She's been trying to find a way into Jackson's life, as soon as he got her a job at City Hall."

'She can have him. It's more than overwhelming though, to learn that Jackson is capable of juggling so many innocent hearts."

"At least, yours isn't shattered, Lexie. It's battered, but you'll survive."

"I can't wait to see what Melissa will say to me, now that she knows I'm out and she may be in."

"Don't forget...Merrill still holds all the aces. Melissa may be out, too."

"True. But Melissa still has the guts to play out her hand to the end and will seek revenge on a cheater. I think Jackson may have met his true match."

"We can only hope," Mandy's smile was genuine.

## Chapter 49

"That was fun! Is that what you've been doing all these years, Dad?"

Marty and Justin couldn't help themselves. They began laughing.

"I would never have thought you had the detective instinct, Merrill," Marty was genuinely surprised that his sophisticated daughter had so enjoyed playing a double agent.

"Maybe I'll open a Private Investigator office," Merrill said. "It feels good to be doing something besides running Benefits and fund-raisers."

"I would never allow you to do it, Merrill. There are other ways to feel good about something. Your boys still need a mother without bullet holes."

"Just joking, Dad. But I'll think of something safer, now that I've had a taste of intrigue."

Merrill had been so involved trying to get out of her marriage with Jackson, then raising her boys by herself, she forgot there was another life. One that was meant for her to live and enjoy.

This adventure was the key, she felt would unlock a new future for herself. She hadn't felt this alive in years

"We may have to let you loose again, Merrill," Justin started to explain. "The trap's been set to see if Jackson was somehow involved in planting the pills in Father Rob's desk drawer. Your father had to suspect Lexie of giving my son pills from my stock, to place in the priest's desk as a set up. He knew the priest would do everything in his power to prevent him from being elected to office, but more importantly, I believe Jackson wanted Father Rob gone, so he could lay claim to the trust fund set up with Lenore at the mission.

I know your father told you about me being related to the priest. I don't know why Jackson thinks this would make him an heir. He must think my days are numbered on the short list."

Justin let this explanation sink in, before he continued with an even more amazing explanation:

"Your father thought Lexie might be taking the pills on her own and selling them on the street to pay for her wedding. But, Lexie and I have a big secret."

Martin smiled as he was now in on the big secret Justin felt able to reveal to Merrill, since she was going to need to know in order to trap Jackson

"The pills I've been allowing my patients to take are extra-strength aspirin. The power of the mind is limitless. If people think they are getting heavy-duty pain killers, they tend to believe their pain is diminished. Placebos can trick the mind into believing the body is healed."

"Wow! That is a shock. Does Jackson know they're only aspirin?"

"That's where we'll need your help, again, Merrill. We need you to ask Jackson to get you some pain pills, for the knee injury you sustained when you fell off your horse last summer."

"I don't have a horse, Dr. Daniels."

"Jackson doesn't know that. He only knows he wants you and he to get together again as soon as possible. He'll do whatever you ask to prove he's worthy of you once again. He will be your Knight in Shining Armor. And when he offers you something to relieve your knee pain, we'll know whether he knows about the pills being fake or not."

"You two have certainly been busy thinking about all this. But, I think I can stomach another visit with Jackson. It's fun being the one in control, turning the tables of the cheater on him, for once. He always thought he could talk and charm his way out of his mis-deeds."

"He must have been in training all his life to be a politician," Martin commented.

"Sadly, a true statement," Justin admitted. "I regret his mother's passing, but I'm also glad she's not here to see how her son is succeeding in becoming the worst he can be."

"That's why I'm also relieved he doesn't have any inter-action with our sons," Merrill said. "Some children are really better off when there's less parental involvement. I'm not looking for a substitute father, either. You and my father have been excellent male role models. So many of their friends have broken families, it's almost the norm, sad as it is. We may be the richest country in the world, but I think other countries have stronger families because they have less to take the place of strong family tics."

"I bet Lenore would second that opinion, Merrill," Martin agreed. "Her work with refugees at the mission brought her to that same conclusion, years ago. As a matter of fact, I'm going to be doing some volunteer work there, as soon as this mystery is wrapped up."

"Won't you be tied up in Court when all this is brought out in the open?"

"I don't think I'll stick around for the court circus. I've been there, knowing who committed a crime, but couldn't produce enough evidence for a jury to conclude guilt without reasonable doubt."

"Lawyers have become experts in making a jury unsure of bare naked truth." Justin said. "That's another reason why I take care of my patients the way I do. Too many drug pushers get away with selling poison because they know how to lawyer up. I save as many people as I can from their grasp. My patients have withdrawn from any drugs they may have been prescribed for pain by others, and they don't even know it.

They're not driving under the influence, or functioning as addicts. They feel good and they won't have to turn to the street for a pill fix, or worse, heroin."

"If Jackson is somehow involved with this pill situation, I'm going to find out one way or another." Merrill stated. "I'm completely with you guys. So, tell me the plan."

"That's my girl!" Martin never felt prouder of his high society daughter. "Listen up, then sweetheart. Justin and I have made up a good one."


## Chapter 50


Jackson was just responding to a text Merrill had sent him, asking him to call her, when Melissa walked into his office.

"I hear you have a job opening. Lexie told me Mandy up and quit. She didn't say why. What happened?"

He knew Melissa would be in the wings, waiting to pounce.

Jackson had prepared a plausible reason to offer anyone who may be asking.

"Mandy was getting angry about my plans to leave the security of my position here to begin campaigning for a higher political office. She wanted out before I became too involved with politics. That's all. I suppose you'd like her position? Is that why you're here. You want me to give you Mandy's old job?"

"Actually, you promised me Lexie's old position…as your girlfriend, if I was successful in performing certain tasks."

"Let's not get ahead of ourselves, Melissa. I'm willing to let you fill in for Mandy, but things have changed with my marriage situation."

"Right. I heard you broke off the engagement with Lexie, so you could get back with your Ex. It's all over Twitter and even in *The News*."

"News travels fast, but that assumption about me and Merrill is a bit premature. We're trying to see if we can work things out for the sake of our children. Lexie understood. I hope you can, too."

"Bullshit."

"You're being harsh, Melissa. I can't offer you a job if you act like you're not backing me up."

Melissa stood perfectly still, staring at this man who had promised her more than a job. She was calculating how she should proceed. She had many tools to get what she wanted. She could be sweet, discreet, sneaky, and crafty. She chose the latter and turned on her self-control mode, to make Jackson believe she was still on his side. After what she did for him, she would have to be very careful to protect herself. There was no way she was going to take the fall for his part in Father Rob Sullivan's death.

"Sorry, Jackson. You know I can fly off the handle at times. But I know you'll do good by me. I know you need Merrill to make your run for office acceptable to backers and the public. That's why you need me to work for you. In the office, here, now, and work for your campaign to help make you elected."

Behind her sweet words, Melissa was planning how she could make sure Jackson paid for his empty promises, and for putting her in danger for a crime that she never should have been involved with.

Melissa turned on her charm. She was more street-smart than Jackson. He might be lacking in morals and ethics, but she knew more about manipulation. She had pulled herself up from her lousy background. It's true, Father Rob had helped, but she had the smarts to work her way into City Hall without getting a college piece of paper like her old friends, Lexie, Mandy, and Leo.

"Are you offering to work for me, then, Melissa?"

"I am. I can start right now, if you want."

"Then, tell them downstairs you're moving out and up," Jackson smiled his most charming.

"Will do." Melissa could be even more charming when she needed to be.

"I may not be here when you return. The first thing I need you to do is call Merrill and set up a dinner date with her for this evening, wherever she wants. Can you do that?" Jackson was testing her. He wanted to know if she could get over his promise to her that she would be his new love interest."

"Of course. No problem. New day, new way. Hey. That could be your campaign slogan," Melissa smiled sweetly.

Jackson came around his desk, closed his door, and kissed her with enthusiasm.

"You know we'll make all our dreams come true, together, as soon as I move on up into the mayor's office." He softy crooned into her ear.

"What about Merrill?"

"Let me take care of the messes. You're the only one who drives me crazy. Don't forget I'm the only one who makes you happy to be a woman. Together…when all is said and done, we'll be a power duo. We can go all the way to Washington, together.

He kissed her with passion, the way she used to like it.

Melissa smiled, outwardly, pretending to be swept off her feet. She knew it was fake. She now knew he was fake. She never tolerated fakeness in others. He had met his match. She would bring him down for promises broken. She was no wimp like Lexie, or her sister, Mandy. They had all grown up in a tough neighborhood. But she, unlike her friends, had retained much of the toughness for survival in her new environment. She also kept in touch with friends who hadn't wanted to leave the old stomping grounds, where getting drunk and or high was the highlight of the day.

Before Melissa left to give notice to her old boss downstairs at City Hall, Jackson held her tightly.

"Just remember, Melissa. The past can be looked at as a means to an end. If that past creeps up to bite me, I'll know where to look for the person who set the dogs free."

Melissa pulled away but was still acting like she was still enamored. "Jackson, I have too much to lose to let loose anything. Most importantly, I never want to lose you."

She left the office, on her way down to her old job in the water department. The look on her face showed a woman on a mission.

There was much planning to do to bring about Jackson's downfall without bringing herself into jeopardy. Melissa was good at this kind of strategizing. In fact, she was great at it.

## Chapter 51

Merrill dressed meticulously for her dinner with Jackson set for 7:00 pm at EB Greens. She wore an elegant jade green sheath with matching earring and pumps. Her long honey-colored hair resembled a Greek goddess's coiffure. She didn't ordinarily dress like this for an early dinner, but this was like dressing up as a character in a play. She was enjoying this immensely.

"I could learn to like playing a double agent," she murmured, as she looked approvingly in her mirror. "I look like the perfect political candidate's wife."

Her script was set, but open to improvisation. Lenore and Harris were also to be part of the scene. They would be having dinner at the same place, same time, and drop by Jackson's table, coincidentally.

Now that she was clear as to what her role was, she looked forward to playing it to the hilt.

Her boys were spending the night at their grandfather's house. They loved spending time with him, as he was the best story-teller in the world. The difference was, his stories were tales of courage and honor, whereas, his son, Jackson's were pure lies.

Someday she might find a person she could trust enough to seriously date. She had plenty of men around her who wanted to, but after one or two dates, she said she was interested in pure friendship. When the men finally realized she meant it, they moved on. She was not the person who wallowed in self-pity and loneliness. She was extremely busy with her sons and her friends, and for now, that was enough.

She added the finishing touch to her toilette by touching her pulse points with her favorite perfume. She remembered how she had once gone to Father Rob for confession, and he had commented and correctly identified the scent. "Chloe?" he asked. She realized he was naming her perfume, not asking her name.

That broke the ice, enabling her to relate her hatred for a husband who had humiliated her and her family through his chronic infidelity. Talking about her anger with the confessor, she concluded that she could no longer live with her husband, even if she forgave him. The breach of trust had been too great. And now, here she was, working as an agent for Karma. It felt good. Damn good.

Her driver picked her up in front of her home, across Delaware Park on Rumsey Rd. The car, the house, the location, her appearance would all be bait for Jackson to woo her as never before.

On the way over to the restaurant, Lenore texted her:
*It's going to be a memorable dinner. Jackson will be served up BS, royally.*
*It's his just desserts, for sure. LOL.* Merrill texted back.

"May I say, you look lovely, Merrill. New date?" Her driver was an old patient and friend of Justin Daniels. He took care of Merrill and the boys' transportation needs in return for room and board in the large house where Merrill lived. His wife was her housekeeper. They had become like members of her family, themselves. Her boys even called Saul, *Uncle,* and Martha, *Aunt.*

"It's an old date, Saul. Thanks for the compliment. I need the big guns out tonight if I'm going to land him."

"Can I ask who the lucky fella is?"

"Actually, it's my ex-husband."

"Oooh-KaaY," Saul replied. "Happy hunting, then."

"Don't worry, I aim to maim, not kill."

# Chapter 52

Melissa had set up the dinner date with Merrill, as Jackson had requested. She was savvy enough to know that a woman scorned, seeking revenge, is her own worst enemy. Even though Jackson had not come through with his promise to make her his leading lady, she had larger worries. She had to protect herself if the authorities found out she was the one who planted the pills in Father Sullivan's desk drawer.

Jackson was the one who had thought up the crazy plan to get rid of the priest and his father, the doctor, with the simple task he had told her to carry out that was supposed to have made both men disappear and clear the way for him to inherit both estates. *By disappear,* he had explained that it was meant to make the priest look like he was a drug-addict, and make his father look like the one who had given him the pills.

"They'll both be arrested, and I can start working on inheriting both their estates."

The plan was for Melissa to walk into the rectory with her friend from the old neighborhood, who was there with her to record the entire sequence of events. Father Rob had never met either of them.

The priest's door was never locked until he left for the evening. He was used to late-night visits by people who had nowhere else to turn.

Jackson had gone over the plan a number of times. It seemed a no-brainer. There was no intention of the priest getting hurt, physically. His reputation was what they were after, and that of Jackson's father.

She realized now, that the plan was full of stupidity. The main thing that galled her was Jackson's role in it could never be proven.

Melissa was to come in with a stash of pills, scatter them on his desk, quickly, before the priest would even know what was going on. He would look surprised, and her friend would start taking pictures on his cell. They would then leave, as quickly as they entered, and send the pictures directly to the news outlets with the caption, *Local priest, found taking and distributing pills, provided to him by his friend, Dr Justin Daniels.*

The reporters would scurry in and find the priest still stunned with the pills scattered around the rectory, trying to explain what had happened. The public wouldn't buy his lame explanation.

An investigation would follow, and both men would be indicted on drug charges. Jackson would then freeze both men's trust funds, and find a way to break into them with his other legal connections. He had enough police officers on the take to make anything look the way he wanted it to.

Jackson found out months ago, that Melissa was using her friendship with Lexie to acquire pills from his father's stock. She told Lexie that she had severe back pain from a car accident and was waiting for an operation, but couldn't bear the pain while waiting for it to be scheduled. That had been a year ago. Lexie had been able to supply her with at least 50 pills a month. Melissa wasn't using them herself, as she had seen first-hand what addiction had done to some of her friends. Her own mother had OD'd. She didn't know or care who her father was.

She had met Jackson one day, while visiting Mandy in Jackson's office. Jackson told her he could certainly help get one of Mandy and Lexie's old friends a job in the water billing office at City Hall.

"That would be great, Mr. Daniels!" Melissa had gushed.

"Give me your number and I'll call you when it's all set up."

"Jackson's one of the few people in City Hall with heart, Melissa." Mandy had said. Now, Melissa realized she had said those words, sarcastically.

"When Jackson called her about the job, he asked if she could meet him to talk over the details. He hadn't wanted her to come to the office, saying it would look to nosy city-hall people as an act of favoritism. He asked if he could drop by her apartment. She agreed.

He came over that evening with pizza and beer. It made her feel comfortable with him. She was confused at first, when he started putting moves on her, subtle at first. A touch on her hand, on her shoulder. Pushing back a strand back of her hair. "You have lovely auburn hair, Missy." She was smart enough to know what was happening, but played naïve.

"Thank you, Mr. Daniels. I know Lexie has some beautiful hair as well. Is that what attracted you to her?"

"Not as much as I'm attracted to you," he said, moving in to kiss her hair. "And you smell so good, too."

"I taste even better...Jackson."

The affair had started that easily. Jackson came to Melissa's apartment when he wasn't courting Lexie, promising her that as soon as he came into some money, he could drop Lexie, and the two of them could set up house.

"The only reason I'm with Lexie is because she's my father's nurse. She even cooks for him. She has access to his books, and finances. I need to know how much money he has, so when he passes on, which may be sooner rather than later, I can plan how to get my share of the estate. I don't want him donating it to some dumb cause."

Aren't you part of the Will, anyway, because of being his only son?"

"It's complicated. We've had some serious falling outs over family matters."

"Then, if you had money, you would drop Lexie in a heart-beat?"

"What do you think? She can't hold a candle to you. You are probably the sexiest woman I've ever met, Melissa."

If he had told her she was the most beautiful, she would have known he was lying. But, he showed her, in many ways, how physically, he was attracted to her. She knew she had him, as many women before her, had gotten their man.

Beauty is nice, but sex is the most powerful aphrodisiac there is. At least, she had thought so. Now she knew money and power were just as equal in attracting and keeping a man's interest. She had the sexual charms, now she needed the money to keep Jackson interested in her, before his father died. She let him in on her plan to acquire plenty tax-free cash, hoping to tie him to her with money.

"I've been using Lexie for my own purpose, too, Jackson. She supplies me to with pills from your father's stock. I'm building up my reserves and plan to sell them to this guy I know from the old neighborhood, for a nice profit, of course."

"How much have you made, so far?"

"In one year, I've made over twenty-grand, under the table." She made twice that amount, but didn't want to reveal too much, till she was more sure she wanted what Jackson had to offer her in exchange.

Jackson whistled, "That's a nice chunk of change."

"To you, it might not seem like that much. To me, it's a 401K"

"Let me think about all this. If you want us to be together sooner, rather than later, I may have a plan to get us there, using the pills you get supplied so freely by Lexie."

A few days later, they worked together on the plan to bring down Jackson's father and the priest- father.

"I know my father's estate will be easier to get to. But, I'll have to think more of how to get my cousin's trust fund set up in my name, instead of the mission's."

"Your cousin?"

"Yeah. Turns out, my father is the priest's uncle. That makes me his cousin."

"How did you find all this out?"

"Your friend, my ex-employee, Mandy, did some investigating. Even the priest didn't find this out till a few days ago. Mandy's gone…so now…you're the keeper of my secrets."

Melissa smiled in her sweetest way, while her mind filed away this important information. She didn't trust Jackson. She hoped he would come through with his promise to marry her though, so she could become the First Lady of Buffalo. That would be the best way to rub it in the faces of all her friends who thought they were better than her because of a shitty piece of worthless paper, called a college diploma.

Melissa was finally able to see that her own self was getting in the way of being successful. She was always trying to use her physical assets to get what she wanted. She thought they had worked on Jackson, in getting a job in City Hall. She thought using her body would get her even further. Now, she finally saw that it was Jackson using her to get himself further.

The question now was, was it too late for her to still turn the tables on him? She had to. Especially now, when she couldn't stand the thought of him anymore.

The plan they had concocted had failed…miserably…and the priest was really dead, and not from a drug over-dose. Melissa had to think carefully how to make it look like a true accident, in case the cops got too close to what had really happened.

Of course, she was sorry it turned out the way it did. She had a conscience. But she also had survival instincts. She wasn't sure, at all, if Jackson was going to throw her under the bus the way he had done before to his ex-wife, and to Lexie, his ex-fiance. She didn't want to be ex'd out by the only other person who knew what had happened. Strike that. There was one other person who knew…the one responsible for the priest's death. And that person could be her ace in a hole, if she needed it.

# Chapter 53

Lenore didn't tell her other friends the plan Martin, Justin, and Merrill had made to entrap Jackson. Lexie had told Justin about giving pills to her friend, Melissa, because she knew they weren't opioids, but aspirin.

"Melissa doesn't have to know that I'm giving her fake drugs. She's like your other patients. She said her pain's bearable since taking the pills, so there's no harm in letting her mind control her pain. I'm not getting any money for them, so if it's fine by you, can I keep her supplied?"

Dr. Daniels agreed. "The more we can keep people off the real stuff, the better. It's too bad they think they need something to make life free of any aches and pains, but so be it. The alternative is way worse."

Lexie continued supplying Melissa with non-addictive pills, knowing they could do no real harm.

Of course, Lenore would tell Shelly and Tina all about what was going on, after the dinner this evening. Harris was in on it, and so was Nicki. But the fewer people who knew, the more chance there wouldn't be any slip ups. Merrill had to play her most convincing role ever. She was a lovely person. Lenore wanted to get to know her better after all was said and done. Right now, it was better if she and Harris behaved like Jackson had their primary interest in making him the next mayor.

Finishing their delicious meal at E.B. Greens, Harris toasted his wife with the promise that they needed to go out to dinner more often, together.

"We've both been so busy, darling, with the needs of so many others…let's try and remember that you and I have spousal needs to get re-acquainted as well."

Lenore smiled gently at her handsome husband, astonished that they had managed to find each other so late in life, but thankful for it.

"I promise, Harris. We have no empty nest to wait for. But we do have to leave our mission nest and be with each other for some exclusive time. I love you, my darling."

"I love you, too, Lenore. Now let's go and finish this scene, as planned."

"While Lenore and Harris were dining, heads were turning to see the striking couple who had just been led to a table by the maître d'.

Some people recognized Merrill from her society work at charitable benefits. A few recognized them from the photo published the previous day in the newspaper. Of course, no one approached them. Their table was in an intimate corner.

When the maître-d pulled out Merrill's chair, she winced with pain.

"Do I detect you're in some pain, Merrill." Jackson sounded sincerely concerned.

"It's nothing. I had a riding accident and tore my knee up some in a fall off my horse. With the crack-down on pain pills, my doctor isn't going to re-new my prescription till next month."

"That's a long time to be in noticeable pain. Maybe I can be of some help. I do have connections."

"I wouldn't dream of you asking your father for some pain pills, Jackson."

"Truthfully, neither would I. But I do know someone who has some pills left over from when she needed them, before her back operation."

"You do?" Merrill was totally immersed in her role.

"She works for me, as a matter of fact. She asked me if she should give them back to her doctor, now that her operation was a success, and she no longer needs them. She says she has some not so nice friends from the old days who would love to get their hands on her prescription."

"Wow. She sounds like an honest person You're lucky to have her working for you. But what happened to you fiance's sister? Wasn't she your secretary?"

"We parted ways after she found out I was serious about us getting back together. She was furious I had told her sister, Lexie, that it was over between us. I really want us to work again as a couple, Merrill."

He looked at her longingly, and gently held her hand in his. It was all Merrill could do to stop herself from pulling it away in horror.

"I know the boys would want us back together again, Jackson." She couldn't help but add, "Of course, they don't really know who you are. You'd have to be introduced to them, slowly."

"I was thinking the same thing, Mer. Remember when I called you that the first time, explaining that in French, *mer* meant the sea. That you had engulfed me in love."

Merrill was silent, pretending it was emotion holding her tongue, when in reality, she had to hold back a gag reflex.

It was shocking to recall how this fake man had won her heart over the objections of her parents. They had seen right through him. She had only seen what he wanted her to see. That was no longer the case. She was trying to make him see, this time, what she wanted him to see. It seemed to be working.

When they were finished with their dinner, they were approached by Lenore and Harris who just happened to be having dinner at the restaurant as well.

"Isn't this a pleasant coincidence?" Lenore beamed. "I was just telling Harris how much I admire the work Jackson's been doing as a comptroller. His talents are being wasted and I was hoping to back him in a run for the mayoral spot this election."

Jackson couldn't get up fast enough. He was floating in happiness.

"This is a very pleasant surprise. Please join us, for an after-dinner cocktail, or dessert."

"Well, if you don't mind? I would like to ask you a favor."

Lenore and Harris were seated when Jackson asked them if they knew Merrill.

"Yes. We met at Father Rob's Memorial Service a few weeks ago. Her father, Detective Foster introduced us. Nice to see you again, Merrill, and this time under more pleasant circumstances. You both know my husband, Harris. He's my silent partner in crime at the mission."

Merrill's eyes grew wide at Lenore's comment. Did she want her to burst out laughing.? This was not a time for joking. Although it was a brilliant way of making everyone comfortable and at ease with each other.

"It looks like the newspapers weren't reporting fake news," Harris said. "If I may intrude on your privacy, are you two thinking of reconciliation?"

Jackson looked lovingly at Merrill. "I think we are, aren't we, darling?"

Merrill looked down at the table and nodded slowly, even shyly.

"This is definitely good news," Lenore stated. "Not only for yourselves and your children, but as I'm sure Jackson has told you, Merrill, since I'm hoping to back him in the next mayoral race. A good family unit is the best strategy for getting votes."

Jackson looked perturbed, but quickly recovered. "I haven't really brought up that possibility, yet, Lenore. I first wanted to see if Merrill would have me back. I didn't want her to think I was only asking her to because of politics."

He stole a glance at his ex-wife trying to judge her reaction.

"I believe Jackson has convinced me he's changed, Lenore. I trust he wants me for me. As a matter of fact, he already broke off his engagement as an honest attempt to show me how serious he is about us getting back together. If Jackson wants to run for a higher office, then I don't see a problem with my backing him, either."

"Really, darling? Oh, you don't know how happy and relieved I am to hear this. I didn't want to even touch on the mayor thing, fearing you might think the old Jackson was back, plotting and conniving."

Merrill had no words. She simply smiled, and patted Jackson's hand in reassurance.

"What was the favor you wanted to ask me Lenore?"

"I almost forgot. It's wonderful to see love re-ignited."

Merrill gave her a stern look. She knew Lenore was enjoying this charade as much as she was, but she didn't want to blow it.

"Harris and I are sponsoring a fund-raiser for the restoration of the Central Terminal in Father Rob's honor. We've almost reached our monetary goal and will be breaking ground soon. It would be the best place for you to make public your announcement of becoming a candidate. Your father has generously donated to the fund. I'm sure he'll be proud of your announcement. Merrill will be at your side, proving that you have strong family ties. There'll be big donors in attendance, as well. They are looking for someone new to push Buffalo further ahead than ever before. Do you think this plan could work for you?"

"Lenore...Harris...I don't know how I can ever thank you for this opportunity. You...and of course, Merrill, are making me the happiest man alive, tonight."

Lenore offered to give Merrill a lift home. Merrill explained she wanted to get home early to see to her boys.

Jackson said he understood and was grateful, as he had a late-night stop to make in order to drop off some important files that needed immediate attention. He was going to swing by his new secretary's apartment to drop them off, and confer with her as to her new duties.

"Thank you, Jackson, for being so understanding. I hope your secretary also has the pain pills I need for my knee. I can't very well campaign with you, hobbling around on a bad leg. Hobbling around would not look very attractive."

Jackson looked at her in alarm. Why did she have to mention the pills.? He quickly made up for her outburst.

"I'm sure she still has those meds. Her back is fine, now, just as you knee will be as soon as you can have it looked at by an orthopedic specialist."

"What's this, now?" Lenore wasn't going to let go an opportunity of seeing Jackson squirm.

"It's nothing more than my secretary having some extra-strength Tylenol she said irritates her stomach. It's a prescription from my father, in fact, that helped her back pain until she had an operation.

Merrill can see if the pills help her with her knee pain until she has it looked at."

"Well, be careful with pill-swapping," Harris advised. "These days, people may not know what they may be putting into their bodies. But, as long as they're from your father, I don't think they'll be harmful."

"Great advice, Harris," Merrill said. "But I hope they work for me. I can barely sleep with the pain."

"I'll be your Knight in Shining Armor, Merrill. From now on, you can count on me." He leaned in for a kiss. Merrill was quick enough to offer her cheek.

"I'll call you tomorrow, Jackson," Lenore advised. "We can plan your announcement before the Benefit. Things will start moving quickly, after that."

"I can't wait," Jackson smiled. He was feeling on top of the world. He looked around the restaurant and saw a few reporters, busily snapping pictures. It was going to be a wonderful morning edition.

# Chapter 54

Lenore and Harris drove with Merrill to Dr. Daniels' home, where Nicki and Martin were also waiting. The car-ride was silent until Merrill was finally able to speak.

"I almost feel sorry for him."

"No need," Lenore explained. "If he has nothing to hide, Harris and I meant what we offered. We'll back him for a mayoral run. If he is guilty, however, of whatever, it's his own damn fault."

"His own father thinks he's into something unethical, Merrill," Harris backed up their promises made at the restaurant. "All we're really doing, technically, is vetting a potential candidate we might wish to sponsor."

"When you put it that way, I don't feel so bad anymore. He looked like a little kid at Christmas, tonight."

"Yes, he did." Lenore admitted. "We only want to find out if a grinch is actually behind his mask of charm."

"I can see now how easily it was for me to be duped by him in the first place."

"Merrill, don't beat yourself up. He's good at being bad. Trust me," Harris said. "I've worked in counter-intelligence to know the very best at subterfuge are those who actually believe that what they're lying about is the truth."

Arriving at Justin's home, Nicki quickly embraced Lenore and Harris. She thanked Merrill for acting like a spy in setting up a trap Jackson might find himself enmeshed in.

"I thought it was fun, at first," Merrill replied. "Now I don't know how my father investigated crimes all these years. It's not really all that much fun."

"How's that?" her father asked.

"It's difficult realizing that people can deceive so easily. Not only for good, like we were, but also for things that may not be so nice. It's untidy."

"That's why I like my work, Merrill. I like tidying up the messes people make not only of their lives, but the lives of other, innocent people."

"By trying to find the truth?"

"Exactly. That's where the work comes in."

"I could get philosophical, being the elder here," Justin said. "I mean, truth can be relative to reality, but not a fixed fact. I'm reminded of the belief people once held as truth that the world was flat, and the center of the universe."

"I have to agree with Dr. Daniels, Merrill. I've found that facts can be presented to a judge and jury, but those facts can be manipulated to present a truth that, to me, is very untrue."

"What about our search for the truth in the matter of Father Rob's murder?"

"Be prepared, Merrill. Even if we prove to ourselves beyond a reasonable doubt how Father Rob died, or who may be responsible for his death, once our evidence gets to court, a jury may be led to believe that the evidence is not proof enough of guilt."

"I have to say what Martin has experienced has been my own experience." Nicki said. "So many times, what I have felt as truth and tried to relate to others, has been explained away as impossible."

"You must be talking about your psychic abilities," Lenore said.

"Yes. And I know Father Rob believed in my abilities, as sure as he believed in God. There's a connection between people's religious beliefs, and their ability to have faith when there is no visible proof."

"We really are getting way too philosophical, here," Martin said. "Right now, Merrill, Lenore, and Harris have set our plan in motion to try and find out if Jackson has any connection between the pills Lexie gave Melissa, and the pills found in Rob's desk drawer."

"He has said he'll get me some of those pills to help me with my made-up knee pain," Merrill said.

"That's the proof we need to see the connection," Justin said. "The pills Lexie gave Melissa, are the ones I give my patients. They're not strong opioids. They're extra-strength aspirin. The police have confirmed to Martin what hasn't been made public: the pills found in Rob's drawer are not opioids, but extra-strength aspirin."

"That shows us," Martin explained, "that there is a connection between Melissa being in Rob's office with those pills. When they were planted there is the question. Now, we're trying to find a connection between Melissa, the pills, and her new boss, Jackson. If she gives him some of those same pills for Merrill's use, we have a connect the dots situation going on."

"Even though that connection is made, that doesn't prove anything, does it?" Merrill lamented.

"No. It means we have a lead," said Martin. "I've followed many dead- end leads, but this one is very promising."

"Are the police going to question Lexie and Melissa, and even Dr. Daniels?" Merrill asked.

"As a matter of fact, all three already have been interrogated, since the pills were reported to have come from Dr. Daniels." Martin admitted.

"Jackson never said anything about that to me," Merrill said.

"He doesn't know," Harris said. "Am I right?"

"Not yet," Martin said, "but as soon as Jackson gives those pills to Merrill, you-know-what will hit the fan."

"Will you be meeting with Jackson, soon, Merrill?" Lenore asked.

"I'll be waiting for his call, tomorrow."

"Do you want someone to go with you, when you meet him?" Nicki asked. "I have a feeling that the situation might be more dangerous than you think."

"Don't worry," Merrill stated, confidently. "I've got this."


## Chapter 55


Nicki's premonition was correct. Jackson went straight to Melissa's apartment after leaving Merrill with Lenore and Harris.

"I need some of those pills you got from Lexie, Melissa."

"What makes you think I have any left?"

"Come on, Melissa. I know you're selling them on the side to your old friends. Even sweet innocent Lexie could have been selling them to pay for our wedding plans. The profit motive is too much to ignore."

"Then, are you suggesting that my character isn't up to par with someone who could resist that kind of temptation?"

"Thank God, it isn't, my sexy woman." Jackson thought appealing to Melissa's sexual nature was his hook into her psyche.

"What happened at dinner tonight with your Ex? Are wedding bells going to be ringing soon?"

"Not if you do as I ask." Jackson said.

"Which is what?"

"Which is simply a re-working of what I had originally planned.

I supply the pills to Merrill to relieve the pain in her leg. She becomes addicted. I publicly state that addiction has even touched my personal life, earning the respect and support of the public. I announce that my close friend, and personal secretary has seen me through this terrible crisis. We end up together."

"How's that again?"

"After Merrill over-doses, we can begin our own public relationship, and this time you'll be my first lady."

"What if the police get to me first? There hasn't been much public leaking of their investigation. I haven't heard a peep from Lexie, although I know she and your father have been questioned."

Jackson was not used to so many questions.

"Just give me the damn pills already."

"I asked you what do I say if I'm questioned by thepolice?"

"Tell them the truth, if they ask. The truth as we see it, that is. You admit you went to the rectory that evening for some personal counseling. On your way out, you saw a friend of yours from the old neighborhood, asking if the priest was still in. You said *Yes* and went on your way home. You were shocked to learn of the priest's death the next day. You suspected that the guy you knew had heard of the pills Father Rob had been using, and demanded them. When the priest refused, he might have threatened him with a gun to his head. It must have gone off by accident, or intentionally.

The guy may have tried to cover it up, by taking some of the pills, and putting the gun in Father Rob's hand to make it look like a suicide. You couldn't go to the police because you were afraid of a revenge killing. You still refuse to name the guy you ran into, because you have no proof that this is what may have happened."

"Wow! You should be a writer. You've twisted just enough true information to make what really did happen get me off the hook, and yourself, as well."

"Exactly."

"But what if they find out who the guy is. There are security cameras surrounding the mission."

"All the better. They'll find him themselves. Who's going to believe the story of some doped up guy from your old neighborhood. He'll simply repeat what happened, but his version will sound concocted, not yours."

"You asked me to scatter the pills on Father Rob's desk, which I did so the guy could take pictures with his cell. So far, so good. I left, but the guy saw the pills, got greedy, didn't take pictures of the startled priest, and wanting the pills for himself., threatened him with a gun. Where did he get the gun, Jackson? I knew this guy, and he may be a drug addict, but he's not a killer."

"Someone may have given him the gun, earlier, as protection."

"Protection? I don't think he even knew how to use one."

Jackson was getting impatient. What was it with all the questions.

"Stop acting like a detective, Melissa. Someone may have told your friend that there was an even bigger stash of pills the priest was hiding and putting the gun to his head would scare and get him to talk. The trigger may have been overly-sensitive, and if there was an accident, the friend, your friend, Melissa, could simply place the gun in the priest's hand to make it look like a suicide."

"Is that what you told him, Jackson?"

"I don't know who told him. Maybe a friend of his. He is a friend of yours, right darling?"

Melissa knew Jackson was threatening her with the possibility that she could be implicated in the disastrous plan he had orchestrated. Why she had agreed to it in the first place was one of the biggest mistakes, thus far, in her life. Thank God, she had other friends besides the one who must have shot father Rob. Thank God, her friends, real friends, Lexie and Mandy had arranged for her to tell the real story to their friend, Detective Foster. She could be granted a plea deal for any part she may have played in the priest's murder. She would gladly accept it, because unlike Jackson, she had a conscience. She didn't want to ask Jackson how he knew which one of her friends was going with her to the rectory. He would know her fishing had gone too far.

"I only have about twenty pills left, Jackson."

"That should be plenty to begin getting Merrill hooked. I'll call her tomorrow to meet me somewhere; probably in Delaware Park across her home. I don't want to see the boys, just yet. No sense getting acquainted with them now. I won't be using their mother too much longer."

Melissa cringed inside, realizing how much more than a sociopath Jackson really was. He had alienated himself from his father, she knew. But his own sons?

"I'll take Merrill to lunch on Elmwood, and make sure she takes at least two of the pills in front of me. I'll call her later that evening to see if they're working. Make sure, you get your hands on more pills from Lexie."

Jackson looked pleased with himself.

"Even I can't believe we're going to get away with this," he bragged.

"We?"

"I admit my plan that you and your friend tried to carry off was kind of dumb. But, this one with Merrill, is going to be less messy, and you won't have a hand in it."

Melissa didn't tell Jackson that she had learned all about him and his lack of human emotion when Lexie and Mandy made a surprise visit to her apartment the day before Jackson took Merrill to dinner. They advised her to tell all she knew to their friend, the detective, who was also Merrill's father. They also told her they were going away for a while, and it was up to Melissa to decide which path she wanted to take: with Jackson, or away from him.

Lexie had told her that the pills she had been given were not opioids, but strong aspirin. That's the proof that would place Melissa in father Rob's office, or at the very least, prove that she was selling fake pills on the side.

Melissa broke down. She admitted Jackson had convinced her to arrange for the pills to be placed in the rectory, making it look like the priest was a drug addict. Her friend from their old neighborhood was supposed to take pictures and send them to the newspaper. He had gotten greedy for the pills though, not in the original plan, and shot the priest, instead.

"Who's the friend, Melissa?" Mandy had asked. "I'm sure Lexie and I know him too."

"He's mixed up with some dealers. I can't tell you his name because he or even I, might be the next to go."

"I'm sure someone will rat him out, especially when they find out the pills he might have been pushing are fakes."

"You haven't been selling them on the street, yourself, have you, Melissa?" Lexie was hoping the answer was negative.

"I haven't, yet. But, I was going to. Thank God, I was saving them up, instead., to make a big sell. I might already be dead, if I had."

"Good luck, Melissa, Mandy said. "I hope you make the right decision. Even jail will be better than a grave."

Melissa was alone with her thoughts for hours. She couldn't sleep at all. When Jackson called the next evening for more pills, she knew what she had to do. She arranged to meet Detective Foster. The rest would be up to him.

There was no way she was going to do nothing while Jackson waltzed around everyone's well-being. She had to take care of herself. And she now knew the best way to do it.

# Chapter 56

The next evening, Lenore asked the Detective to meet with her and the other women at Tina's.

"After explaining to me what happened, I want the women to see for themselves. You said the coverage would be on the six o'clock *TV News.* Tina's loft is one of our favorite places. Rob so enjoyed it when Tina prepared one of his favorite home-cooked meals for us all. Tina really misses cooking for him."

"I think I could be just as receptive a gourmand as the good priest."

"I asked Tina to prepare his favorite pork chop dinner for us. She was thrilled. We'll tape the *News.* I already prepared the women that the News special will be our dessert. That there was something on it, we needed to watch over and over again. They were curious, thinking it was some celebrity who had agreed to come to the Benefit we're planning for the renovation of the Central Terminal. You told the News outlet to hold the special segment till the very end of its broadcast so I hope no one leaks the info."

"I've found the reporter to be very discreet in the past, so I don't think we'll have a problem. All that's been announced is a special report on the opioid crisis in our city."

"We'll watch the Special together, Martin, and be able to reflect on all that's happened, sitting out on Tina's deck. Lake Erie has always been one of our favorite back-drops for sharing, feelings, and now, facts. You can answer the million questions, I'm sure everyone will have."

"Then it's a good thing I'll be fortified with a delicious dinner."

"I know Dr. Daniels and your daughter, Merrill, have already been given all the facts. I think the story coming from you, will be less complicated for all of us, if we hear it together."

"That makes a lot of sense, Lenore. I'm sorry we won't even be going to Court, despite all the facts we now know. As happens more often than not, concrete evidence is lacking. People can and do get away with murder. But, once everyone knows what truly happened, they'll feel some closure. That's all I can offer. I'm getting worn out by cases with no convictions. But, justice has its own special agent at times like this. Karma can always be counted on."

"I'm sure Nicki would agree. But it might be better for us all if we could witness Karma in action."

"Someday, we may. We just have to have faith."

"That's something Rob would say, for sure, Martin."

# Chapter 57

The banter was light and frivolous when the women met up at Tina's. They weren't surprised to see Martin Foster there. He already started doing volunteer work at the Mission. Lenore had invited him, telling Tina he had a wonderful appreciation for home-cooked meals, just as Rob had had.

"Don't think you're so clever, Lenore, that we haven't been brain-storming about why you want us to watch a News Special together," Shelly commented.

"Yeah." Tina agreed. "We know you've managed to convince some celebrity to appear at the Benefit for the Terminal."

"I think it may be someone like Regis Philbin, who can entertain an audience by regaling them with anecdotes," said Nicki.

"I never thought of him," Lenore admitted. "He would have been perfect, except I don't think the younger donors would have been that excited to sit and listen to someone from our generation."

"Then you admit, it! We'll be learning about someone you managed to commit to our Benefit. Someone famous that young people may know." Shelly believed she was getting closer.

"Is it a singer? A movie star? A reality star?" Tina was growing intense.

"Please," Nicki implored, "Don't tell us it's a politician."

The women groaned in unison, when Lenore was silent. They believed her silence meant a *Yes*.


"Did you enjoy Tina's dinner, Martin?" Lenore asked innocently.

"Magnifique, Tina. I'm almost speechless in my ecstasy. How can anyone make pork chops so tender and tasty?"

"That's exactly how Rob would have responded," Tina said with a tinge of sadness. But she was pleased that Martin had noticed and appreciated her culinary efforts.

"You know he's still hanging around the earth plane, till all this gets straightened out," Nicki stated. "Have faith."

# Chapter 58

"Time to reward faith, then ladies," Lenore announced. "It's time we watched the News Special. It's going to be something, just like I promised. Please hold your comments and questions till the very end. Martin will answer all we can throw at him." The women gathered around the large screen. Tina started the recording. The room was silent as the News Commentator began:

*The events of this afternoon, show how desperate opioid users and illegal sellers in our own community have become. They will lie, steal, and worse yet, murder in the hopes of getting their next high. Sellers place money above human decency and lives. And that high or greed comes at a cost to the innocent.*

*The innocent, in this case, was Reverend Robert Sullivan.*

Hoping to score a large amount of addictive pain pills, a lone addict walked into the priest's office and asked him where he was hiding the pain pills he believed the priest had. The priest must have told him all he had was a drawer full of plain aspirin.

In desperation, a gun was put to the priest's head to force him into revealing where the real pain pills were hidden. The gun went off, either accidentally, or on purpose. Some of the pills were scooped up when the addict tried to make the shooting look like a suicide, before he fled the office. Father Rob's body was discovered by Lenore Burns, the next morning.

An innocent victim was taken by opioids, even if he wasn't using them himself. Police confirmed that the pills found scattered on the desk were high dosage aspirin.

Our story grows to expand into places we had once trusted as safe.

This afternoon, police stopped a vehicle speeding through the section of the Scajaquada Expressway that has a speed limit of 30 mph.

The driver was asked to step out of his car. He tried to explain he didn't realize he had been speeding and worked at City Hall. One of the Officers recognized him, but still asked to search the vehicle, because of the excessive speed the man was driving, clocked at 65mph. A bag of oxycodone was found, under the driver's seat. There was no accompanying prescription. The driver said he had no idea it was there.

"Someone must have planted it there. It might be one of my political enemies who knew I was going to announce my run for mayor of Buffalo next week, and is trying to set me up to fail."

*"It wasn't planted there, sir. We received a tip to be on the look-out for your vehicle. It was reported that you were going to attempt to sell the pills."*

*"That's outrageous!" the man shouted forcefully in denial.*

*He was taken to the station, where he was booked with intent to sell an illegal substance.*

*The man is out on bail, but his career has been destroyed. His run for mayor has been curtailed. Charges are pending. So, until an investigation is complete, only Father Rob Sullivan's name can be used in this special report.*

*Another potential victim of opioids has been spared, thanks to an anonymous tip. Luckily, the person, who was stopped by the police while speeding to sell the pills he had stashed under his seat, has been prevented from making another person a victim, safe, for now. The pills he had were laced with deadly fentanyl.*

*If you believe you or your family is safe from the effects of these deadly pills, think again. It's almost as if some foreign enemy has arranged for us to meet our downfall through using them., or being its innocent victims, like Father Robert Sullivan, the would- be mayor of Buffalo, or the poor addict who killed Father Rob, for a handful of aspirin.*

*This is John Jacobs, signing off, from a special report on the crisis facing our families, our communities, and our nation.*

The Special ended with a number to a hot-line to call if anyone had tips or was in need of drug counseling for themselves or others.

Martin looked around at the startled faces on the silent women, staring at the empty TV screen, trying to wrap their minds around what they had just seen.

"What have we just watched?" Shelly was the first to ask. "Did we just find out how and why Rob was murdered?"

"And did we just find out who did it?" Tina asked.

"The un-named man in the report? Is it who I think it is?" Nicki said, more than asked.

"Let's sit on Tina's deck," Lenore instructed. "We'll answer these questions first. Martin can make everything you've heard, clearer than I ever could."
"This isn't the dessert I was imagining," Tina stated. "I'm thinking this more like a main course."
"Then we'll dig in until all are satisfied," Lenore gently smiled. She knew her friends would be upset. But, at least they would know why and who was to blame.

# Chapter 59

Merrill sat with Dr. Daniels, watching the News Special. She wasn't as shocked as the other women had been, because she knew that her ex-husband was a twisted person.
"How can a son, you've raised, turn out to be so lacking in human kindness, concern, and compassion?"

"Unfortunately, I knew many years ago that Jackson didn't possess the qualities that make a person a decent human being. The only thing that excites him is not human inter-action, but the thrill of power. Money makes people powerful. That's why he has always tried to make more of it, and not through honest work."

"How did he become so unfeeling?"

"There's no explanation I can think of. The brain is still unchartered territory. We don't know what makes people tick. Some think it's a combination of nature and nurture. There is, to my knowledge, no medicine that can make people behave like loving human beings."

"May I ask when you knew for certain that Jackson was lacking human empathy?"

"You found out when you married him. I found out when I married his mother and brought him into my household."

Justin then told Merrill the story he had told Martin, her father: How Jackson wasn't his biological son, and how he had been one of the reasons his son, Charlie, wasn't alive anymore.

Merrill was stunned by this sad story.

"Why couldn't you have warned me before I married him," Merrill asked, somewhat angrily.

"My dear woman, did you believe you own parents when they warned you about him?"

Merrill asked whether Lexie was warned.

"There are no words of warning that would ever convince someone's heart to believe something evil of the person he or she is in love with. It's madness, I know, but, unfortunately, the only way to find out is through personal experience. And even then, some poor souls still refuse to believe it and stay forever. You were wise enough to get out, even though it must have been painful."

Merrill couldn't deny she had been thoroughly as much in love with Jackson, as she was now out of love with him.

"What happens next?"

"Martin told me that because the evidence couldn't pin Father Rob's murder, directly on Jackson, he'll get away, scot-free. He'll maybe get some probation for the opioid possession, but that's it."

"And the addict who did the shooting?"

"Another unsolved case will be filed. No one's going to rat out the guy."

"That's not justice!" Merrill shouted. "How can we get real justice?"

Justin sighed. "We do the best we can with what we know. Justin won't get Lenore's backing for mayor. He won't be named an heir to my estate, and he certainly won't be able to break into Father Rob's Trust Fund. Ultimately, he'll be a middle-aged man, without the power he was so willing to do anything for. I would label this karmic justice."

"What do you think he'll do, instead?"

"Honestly, I think he'll run away someplace and try to start over. There's nothing here for him to plot about. He's already abandoned his own children. I bet he's going to go out West, or even Canada, and find some rich woman, or even man, to seduce with his charm."

"In other words, he's free to do whatever he wants, after ruining the lives of so many others."

"I choose to think of those lives of being free...of Jackson. Don't you think?"

"But Father Rob's dead, because of him."

"He didn't kill the priest, Merrill. But he was able to use his wiles and get an addict to do the killing. No addict...no murder. I believe Jackson is smart enough to keep his own hands free of blood. He knows his most powerful tools are his ability to manipulate others."

Merrill agreed with this final analysis.

" Let's call your father now, and see if his explanation to Father Rob's friends was as satisfactory as I hope mine was to you."

# Chapter 60

Even though the women were angry and upset that Jackson would most likely go free, they wanted to know about the addict who had fired the gun that actually killed their friend.

"No one's going to turn him or her in for fear of retribution from the street dealers who worked for or with him or her."

"Do you think it could possibly be a woman?" Tina refused to believe it might.

"What do you believe, Nicki?" Shelly asked. "Do you have any feelings about the entire situation?"

"I have to agree with Martin that there is no concrete evidence that will persuade a jury to find a guilty verdict for Jackson. The addict that we believe shot Rob, will most likely get his or her just rewards when the street head honchos find out the pills he might have sold them to are merely high dosage aspirin. Street justice will take care of the real killer."

"Do you think Rob is still on the earth plane?" Lenore asked Nicki.

"I still feel his presence, although not as strongly. He might be satisfied that we're satisfied, even though unhappy in knowing what actually happened. I believe he would never want us to spend our remaining days wondering and wasting them trying to find out who killed him and why. I'm hoping he'll give us a sign that it's time for us to move on."

"We still do have a lot of organizing to do before the next Benefit for the restoration of the Terminal," Lenore admitted.

"That was his primary goal," Tina said. "We'll get that job done, and maybe we'll feel him with us as we plod on, even though we won't be able to see or talk with him."

"Why not?" Nicki replied. "We won't see him, of course, in his bodily presence, but I'm sure he'll be felt in every situation he wants to be in."

"But what about leaving this earth plane for his own heavenly reward.?" Shelly wasn't having the possibility that Rob might be stuck here on earth, because of them.

"Let's say that, now, he won't feel the need to be here any longer, but may pay us a visit now and then to see how we're doing. After all, we haven't got life-times, ourselves, to enjoy for many more years." Nicki was explaining the after-life in practical terms.

"Then we'd better start rolling up our sleeves and forget about trying to bring Jackson and the killer to earthly justice," Lenore stated. "What do you think, Martin?"

Before he could answer, his cell pinged a new message. It was from Melissa.

*Looks like Karma came through. The shooter was killed this morning by a hit and run. No need to name him. The police will issue his identity this evening. Jackson has disappeared from the Buffalo area. There is a warrant out for his arrest as he jumped bail. I've decided to join my friends Lexie and Mandy on a Caribbean Cruise. You can reach me in a few weeks, when we return to begin new lives.*

Martin smiled broadly.

"Are you smiling because you're anticipating the apple pie Tina made us for dessert?" Lenore asked. "It certainly smells heavenly."

"What pie?" Tina asked. "I didn't bake anything for today, but it sure smells like I did."

They all stared at Nicki, searching for an explanation.

Nicki's reply gave them the closure they so desired. "This is our message of good-bye, my dear friends. Our dearest Rob is happy, satisfied, and has sent us all the aroma of contentment. You were correct in calling it heavenly, Lenore."

They remained on Tina's deck, over-looking the Lake, looking at the stars, wondering which one Rob was passing on his way to his new home.

## Five Years Later


Lenore looked out at the crowd filling in the newly appointed concourse in the renovated Central Terminal. She was supported by Tina and Shelly on her right, and Harris and her twin, Jaime on her left.

*Thank you all so much for joining us at this memorable occasion. Some of you were here at the start of this journey. We gathered to remember the life of our beloved, Reverend Robert Sullivan five years ago. It was his dream to renovate this magnificent building and help it become what it is today.*

*Thanks to his generosity, and the generous donations of so many listed in our Program, Father Rob has proven that wishes, dreams, and prayers, can become reality.*

*Before we dedicate this wonderful building, I would like to pause and set aside a moment of silence to remember the ones who have joined Father Rob in heaven. They have passed quietly from our planet, but their work and dedication to our efforts will never be forgotten.*

*A silent heartfelt tribute to of course, Father Sullivan, and his friends who are now with him: Dr. Justin Daniels, our dear friend, Nicki Kent and her husband, Lowell. I'm sure they are deciding whether.to stay put for a while, or venture to earth for another turn at life. Those of you who had the pleasure of knowing Nicki, know she believed in re-incarnation. Her strong belief in an after-life has brought many of us comfort.*

*To all the patrons listed in the program who have also passed on, your generosity has made all this a wonderful reality. We know your spirits are here with us. And as proof of your presence...I'm sure we will all be experiencing the aroma of just-baked apple pie. That's Father's Rob's message to us that he is near.*

*We are also grateful to our newly elected Mayor, Merrill Foster. She has seen us through all the red tape government can produce.*

*Together, we have overcome sadness, grief, obstacles, and disappointments and stand in a place built for new travels and home-comings. So now, let us raise our glasses and toast the new Central Terminal, aptly re-named: **St. Michael the Archangel Community Terminal,** in honor of Father Rob, who was a guardian angel to so many. His dream will continue in this building to train, tutor, and teach all who want to rise above, and create new successful journeys.*

Lenore completed the tribute and dedication. Her friends gathered around and reminisced about all that they had experienced during the five years of re-hab.

"Who would have thought I would run for Mayor and win," Merrill said proudly. "Thanks to you and Harris, Lenore, I would never have thought such a prospect was possible. I am thoroughly dedicated to making Buffalo the best it can be. Thank you, for believing in me."

Tina and Merrill' s father, Martin joined in. "Who would have thought your old dad would ever marry again, Merrill?" Tina was beaming as she took Martin's arm. They had been married four years.

"I'm thrilled with the renovation," Shelly also glowed. "The apartments on the top floor are completely full of comfort and charm. The views are outstanding!

My niece is opening a workshop on the second floor, above the offices. She and her husband will lease one of the apartments. Now that she's pregnant, she wants to be close to the design shop of C&V Fashions. Leo is assisting Carlos manage the other shops in Black Rock and at the Mission."

"We're ready to begin renovating the next block of homes, next week," Harris said. "We've demolished two of the blocks already that were simply loaded with dilapidated houses and will begin excavating for the community park in that space, planned for next year."

"I want to stop at the Broadway Market before we go home, Harris," Lenore said. "There's a new cheese shop that opened there. I want to show my brother, Jaime, all over the neighborhood. He can't believe how it's changed. He's even extending his visit from London to enjoy our beautiful Buffalo summer."

The newly refurbished clock in the concourse began chiming 6-o'clock. When the chimes ended, people looked around in wonder. The unmistakable aroma of freshly baked apple pie wafted deliciously through the air, enveloping them in comfort and contentment.

**THE END**

47655089R00150

Made in the USA
Middletown, DE
31 August 2017